REVELATION:

God & Satan In The Apocalypse

By JAMES KALLAS

BOOK STUDY GUIDE by Stephen B. Knudsen

Imagine for a moment that you are back in the classroom--either because you have to be or you want to be. How much you learn is likely to be affected by which case it is for you. Let's suppose you chose the course because you expected to learn something interesting or useful to you, or both. You sit there determined to have an open mind, listen carefully, take good notes, ask for clarification of points that are not clear to you or call for additional information, debate points you question, and become excited by new learnings. After the class is over, you are ready to reflect on what you heard, dig for further information, and wrestle with the question, "What does it mean for me?"

Having purchased this book, you *are* back in a classroom; a professor is about to speak to you. You have paid a very reasonable tuition. A book has some definite disadvantages: the lecture allows the professor to emphasize and explain his main points; the student who asks for it has access to much additional background information (a professor *never* tells in a lecture all he knows); and there is value in hearing and taking summary notes.

But a book has advantages, too: you can learn at your own convenience and in the amount of time you select; you can get instant replay any time you wish; and it provides you with complete and accurate notes (you can quote *exactly* what the author said).

If you are using the book in a small discussion group, the guide provides some assistance in keeping you on the subject. Man is a social animal and usually finds it more comfortable to share new insights and experiences with others. Think how it would be to play golf and hit a hole-in-one with no one else around! A study guide can be viewed as a substitute for a classroom setting if you are reading the book alone. It gives you contact with someone else who is also reading the book.

Getting Ready to Learn

In educational circles today there is talk about "creating an environment" in which learning can take place--or about "building an approach" toward a subject. Our youth would probably call it "getting psyched-up." Learning requires preparation. Our minds need to reach toward the subject under discussion, expecting new information and enlightenment.

You might now be saying, "I saw the title of the book, was interested in Revelation, so I bought it. Isn't that enough?" That's a good beginning, but there is more to be considered. How much do you know about the last book in the Bible called Revelation? What do *you* think it means? For many people (and some religious writers) there is at least a question as to whether this book really does hold some hidden glimpses into the future, or even what present-day events mean. If God has given some hint as to the outcome of present events, we who are his people certainly don't want to miss out on this "inside" information.

If you expect Dr. Kallas' book to be a great new word on the interpretation of present and future events, you will be disappointed. Dr. Kallas suggests that if that is what you expect you should take the book back to your bookseller. I, however, would much rather have you change your expectations and read the book carefully! This book is about Revelation, apocalyptic literature in general, God and history, interpretation of the Scriptures. These are difficult subjects. If only one of them arouses your curiosity and serves as motivation for approaching the book, you will have a pleasant and rewarding experience.

About This Guide and Its Use

Don't let this study guide scare you. Dr. Kallas' book is not so complicated that it needs a special road map to get you through it. There are guides in other books too. This guide is a tool and not your master.

For each section of the book, this guide will furnish:

1. Capsule summary
2. Questions for clarification and discussion

For individual use. The capsule summary may be used as an "appetizer," and the questions for your own reflection on Dr. Kallas' book and the book of Revelation. Do I even dare mention that you should be reading Revelation along with Dr. Kallas' discussion of it? Well, you should!

It would be worth the effort to encourage one of your friends to read this book too, so that you have someone to share it with. We're always looking for good topics of conversation anyway. If you have seen a film lately, try discussing it with someone who also viewed it, and then try to discuss it with someone who hasn't even heard of it. How do the two "discussions" compare? I'm so confident of the outcome that I can say: the same is true with books.

Alternate suggestion: there is a simple study pattern based on three questions: 1. What does it say?
2. What does it mean?
3. What does it mean to me?

You might try using that formula on both Revelation and Dr. Kallas' book, and lay this study guide aside.

For group use. Most groups need a leader, and leaders need group members who do the assigned reading--this seems to be the minimum commitment that can be made. It would also seem reasonable to expect the leader to be at least one lesson ahead of the group, and better if the leader has read the entire book before the sessions start.

Remember that a study guide should not shape your session experience. Often instructions from the outside (such as a study guide) destroy a group's creativity. You will undoubtedly bring to life sharper and clearer statements of the issues and themes than are presented here. Make notes in your copy of Kallas' book and this study guide of your own observations and questions. Each participant needs to wrestle with the question, "How can we best bring these issues to life and make them relevant for each other?"

The group has some decisions to make at the initial meeting. How many sessions are we going to have? When can we meet? Where? Is a leader already chosen, or do we do it? Are the sessions to be for a specified length of time, or is the group willing to have them go on and on? Be careful not to make commitments that will eventually put strain on the group. Most people like to finish what they start. Too many or too lengthy sessions may find other commitments causing frustrations.

The guide provides a plan for six sessions. Scan it to note that Session 1 is organizational, creating an approach to the study. The other sessions group chapters and deal with themes.

The end of each session should be used to build an "approach" toward the next section to be studied.

Session 1

REVELATION: GOD AND SATAN IN THE APOCALYPSE

Preface

Capsule. The resurgence of interest in the book of Revelation stems generally from a "natural curiosity for knowing future events...." More specifically, this interest grows out of pessimism over man's ability to cope with the forces that surround him. Many theologians see in Revelation a promise that in the future God will act and overcome the hostile forces that control us now. Kallas asserts "that life does have a meaning. We are not to despair or dissolve in a puddle of anxiety which sees sorcerers and witches on all sides. We have no need to peer forward into time to see the hand of God--for the hand of God is present even now, shaping and molding our days" (p. 17).

Questions. (1) What do you think the book of Revelation means? Does it refer specifically to events of the 20th century? Are certain scriptural prophecies being fulfilled today? Are we living in the "end times"? (2) If you are familiar with the message of any millennialist theologians (theologians who believe that books such as Revelation are books of prophecy whose riddle can be solved so that present and future events can be explained or predicted), can you remember any of their specific predictions? (3) Kallas suggests that the optimistic view of man's future, prevalent a few years ago, is being replaced by a growing pessimism. Do you agree? (4) Explain the slogans "the God of the gaps"

(p. 9), and "God is Dead...Man is Alive" (p. 9). Can you think of a slogan to describe the situation today? (5) Why do you want to read Kallas' book? What do you expect to learn?

Session 2

Chapter 1: FOUR VIEWS ON REVELATION

Capsule. Four ways of interpreting Revelation have emerged: (1) It describes the end of history (If only we could figure out when the end begins!). (2) It describes the entire period of history from the time of Jesus to the end of time (If only we could figure out where we are now on that time line!). (3) It describes the universal struggle between the good and evil forces of all ages. (4) It describes *a* period of history already past, about A.D. 100. Kallas suggests that our most important question about Revelation is "What did the book mean to the people who first read it?

Questions. (1) Discuss the four views of Revelation, noting positive and negative aspects of each, if you can. (2) "*All* of the books of the New Testament find their first and most significant meaning in the lives of the first people to read them." Do you agree? (3) Does this stance destroy the meaning and usefulness of the New Testament books for people living today? (4) Now that you know that Kallas is going to give you a history lesson before discussing the pages of Revelation, are you willing to continue?

Session 3

Chapter 2: "REVELATION"--MEANING OF THE WORD

Capsule. Revelation is part of a type of literature known as "apocalyptic." This style of Jewish writing first emerged about 586 B.C. during the time of intense persecution under King Nebuchadnezzar of Babylon, and had its greatest flurry about 170 B.C. during an even more intense and bitter persecution by Antiochus Epiphanes, a Persian King. There are some common characteristics in this type of literature. (1) Satan is in control of the world. (2) God will finally destroy the devil. (3) It was always written in symbolic language to disguise its real meaning from all but the eyes of the faithful. (4) It was always written under a fictitious name. The faithful Jews living at the time it was written were able to see through the disguise and understand the message. We're not so fortunate today!

Questions. (1) What does the word "apocalypse" mean? From what you now know of the book of Revelation, would "Apocalypse" be a more fitting title? (2) Describe the type of political situation which gave rise to apocalyptic literature. What was its basic message? (3) Note the "bonus" on pages 39-41, describing the origin of the Sadducees and Pharisees and the Essenes. How do they differ? (4) Kallas says (p. 48), "Certainly it is true that God indeed could lift up a man and reveal to him the secrets of the far distant future and give us relief maps of 20th century political science if he so wished! But *would* he?" What do you think? (5) Is the contention that certain portions of apocalyptic literature cannot be exactly understood by us today acceptable to you? (6) What was the historical situation when Revelation was written? (Read Chapter 3 of the paperback to find out.)

Chapter 3: JOHN, DOMITIAN, AND PATMOS

Capsule. John's later years were lived under Roman persecution of the Christian church because it would not submit to emperor-worship. Exiled, John adopted the style of apocalyptic literature to deliver a message of hope to the discouraged Christians facing the persecution and wondering "Whose world is this: God's or Satan's?" The book of Revelation must be read as an affirmation that "It is *God*, not Satan, who rules the world and stands behind the suffering of the elect on the mainland" (p. 63).

Questions. (1) What was the theological dilemma faced by the Christians John was writing to (p. 56)? Under what circumstances have you faced a similar problem? (2) Examine the passages Kallas refers to, Revelation 14:1,3; 20:2-3, noting his explanation. Can you think of other scripture passages which become difficult if taken literally? (3) Now that you have your Bibles in hand, you're ready for the next four chapters of Kallas' book.

Session 4

Chapter 4: LETTERS TO THE SEVEN CHURCHES

Capsule. The first three chapters of Revelation (read them) set the stage. Confronted with persecution, the Christians are wondering why God is not ruling. John affirms that God is ruling, and that the sufferings they are enduring must be seen as the work of God. God is not only the final deliverance; he works in the present--even in persecution--to refine and purify his people. Repentance, not self-pity, is called for. "The judgment having been spoken, the punishment can now begin" (p. 72).

Questions. (1) Why were seven churches singled out? (2) What are common themes in each of the seven letters? (3) What common pronouncements might God make on all churches today? What might he specifically say to your congregation? (4) How do you feel about John's assertion that God rules over a suffering world, and that he uses suffering to reform and purify his people?

Chapter 5: THE FOUR HORSEMEN--AVENGERS SENT BY GOD

Capsule. To a church that was saying, "Why should such misfortune befall nice people like us?" came John's insistence that they weren't so nice, and that God would punish the church in order to cleanse it. Chapters 4-11 of Revelation (read them) reiterate that theme, assuring the people that God has not forgotten his love for them.

Questions. (1) Kallas many times uses the statement "things are not what they seem." What does that mean to you now? (2) In Chapter 11 it appears that John spotted an error in his logic: if God wishes to purge his church, why must the suffering be universal? What answer does he give?

Session 5

Chapter 6: THE WAR IN HEAVEN--SATAN AN ENEMY?

Capsule. Two problems arising in Revelation, Chapter 12 (read it) are discussed. (1) The people, at the brink of despair, believe Satan is in control and causing the suffering of the churches (apocalyptic thought). Dr. Kallas indicates that John, however, believes that even now God is in command, "Satan is not an independent force, but a tool..." (p. 90). God always reigns. (2) Kallas writes that although Chapter 12 does use the style and language of apocalyptic thought, the *content* of this chapter is in direct conflict with apocalyptic thought. John is saying that not even the enemies of God are in the deepest sense enemies.

Questions. (1) Kallas suggests that John viewed Caiaphas, Pilate, Judas, Rome, and Satan as "instruments of God's plan." What do you think? (2) Are our enemies of today God's agents? (3) Take each problem that Kallas raises and discuss his conclusion. (4) Who is in control of this world?

Chapter 7: CLEANSING COMPLETED--PARADISE RESTORED

Capsule. The theme of God purging his church is picked up again in Chapter 13 to the end of Revelation. John says the persecution comes to an end; Rome is not the power--God is. Those remaining firm in their faith will own the glories of heaven.

Questions. (1) Review the 13 summary statements (pp. 95-99). Do they conform to your observations? Do any need to be reviewed? (2) After the storm comes the sun. What descriptions of the reward to the faithful does John give in the final three chapters? (3) Have you felt that your faith was tested? Was suffering your teacher? (4) Genesis 50:15-21: What was Joseph's attitude toward suffering? Is it the same as John's?

Session 6

Chapter 8: GOD AND SATAN--SOME BIBLICAL VIEWS COMPARED

Capsule. Two final issues are discussed. (1) How can two opposite views of who--Satan or God--is in charge of this present age with its evil and suffering exist side-by-side in the Scriptures? Kallas suggests that the key to understanding this is to understand the difference between Hebrew and Greek languages. The Greek tradition (our tradition) thinks in logical and consistent terms; the Hebrew tradition, on the other hand, thinks paradoxically, and is able to hold opposites together in tension. (2) What comfort can be found in the Revelation portrait of a God who causes woe? Kallas, following the reasoning of his answer to the first question, affirms that suffering can be positive, and can produce positive results. "God does act now--and in the future. Suffering can be good--or evil...and the synoptic Gospels stress one side, whereas John emphasizes the other" (p. 122).

Questions. (1) Do you understand the contrast made between Hebrew and Greek thought patterns? (2) Who is in control of present suffering? Satan or God? In what respects is each answer true? (3) Reference to other passages are scattered throughout this chapter. Use these references to reinforce your understanding of Hebrew paradoxical thought. (4) 1 Peter 1:3-9: which side does Peter seem to emphasize here? (5) If you have viewed the film *Fiddler on the Roof*, discuss Tevye's soliloquies where he wrestles with decisions ("on the one hand...on the other hand..."). Does this help you understand the paradoxical nature of Hebrew thought? (6) On page 122 Kallas raises and answers the question of Scripture being in conflict with itself. How do you feel about this answer? (7) What has this study of Revelation meant to you? What issues has it raised? Has it resolved the issues to your satisfaction, or are there some points that need further clarification for you? (8) What might you say to a millennialist who says that the end is going to come in 1978? (Do you dare try some role play with this question to pull together your understanding of the purpose and content of Revelation?)

REVELATION:

God & Satan In The Apocalypse

REVELATION:

God & Satan In The Apocalypse

By JAMES KALLAS

AUGSBURG PUBLISHING HOUSE

Minneapolis, Minnesota

TO DARLEAN

Partner in pleasure and pain

REVELATION:

GOD AND SATAN IN THE APOCALYPSE

Library of Congress Catalog Card No. 73-78268

International Standard Book No. 0-8066-1332-7

MANUFACTURED IN THE UNITED STATES OF AMERICA

CONTENTS

PREFACE

There is a resurgence of interest in the book of Revelation today. The book, often ignored in the past, has seen a bundle of commentaries written on it in the last few years. This popularity of Revelation today is due at least in part to the insatiable curiosity regarding the future, the interest in the unknown tomorrow, which characterizes the restless human spirit, for most of the books now appearing on the shelves are written precisely in that vein, claiming that in the pages of Revelation we can see the signs of the present times and thus predict the tomorrows. To pull back the veil and to claim to lay bare the future is to attract an audience, for that is the nature of man—fascination with the future! And that is the thrust of the spate of books now appearing, almost all of them claiming to be able to unravel the events about to unfold. Man reveres the past, but he is intoxicated by the heady wine of prophecy, the promise to unlock the hours ahead. The very claim, then, of these many books—that they can reveal to us things which are soon to come—helps to explain the popularity of these books on Revelation.

But this natural curiosity for knowing future events cannot be the sole reason for the popularity of books about Revelation today. That curiosity was part of man's makeup a decade ago as well, and books were not written then about Revelation, at least not in the same measure that they are now. Why, then, this renewed interest now?

The answer rests perhaps in this fact. As little as a decade ago we were riding the crest of an optimistic anthropology, quite convinced that man was a giant, master of his own fate, captain of his own destiny. We were impressed with the marvels of modern technology, nearly hypnotized by the incredible advances of science. Heart transplants were accomplished, the scourge of polio was ended, promising new leads in the fight against cancer were apparently at hand. And, coupled with those things, impressive enough in their own right, were perhaps the even more incredible advances of the space age. Men were walking on the moon! Not long ago, man was unable to fly, and today he can soar to outer space. The modern 747 airplane sits longer, nose to tail, than the original flight of the Wright brothers! Charles Lindbergh, the first man to fly the Atlantic, is alive to watch men conquer the moon! The enormous advance of science, literally exploding in our own day, produced an overwhelming sense of powerful optimism—man is a giant, able to do all things!

It is precisely that technological advance which produced the religious literature of a decade ago. A decade ago men were not writing about Revelation. They were writing instead that "God is dead." That was the catchword of the 1960s. And if one would grasp what was really being said by that phrase, "God is dead," the best thing to do would be to throw away the phrase and substitute for it this one, "Man is alive!" For that was the basic affirmation being made–God was dead, God could be set aside, because mighty man was alive! He no longer needed God to explain all things or conquer unknown terrors. In an older, simpler age we believed in what the theologians call "the God of the gaps." Wherever there was a gap in our knowledge, unable to be explained in any other way, we would resort to God to explain those things. What science could not explain, religion was called upon to elucidate. The primeval savage roaming the jungle floor would see lightning split the heavens and hear the roar of thunder and, being able to explain it no other way, he would say that it was the voice of God. "The God of the gaps" system uses religion to explain what otherwise could not be known. But today we do not need religion to explain thunder. We know that thunder is a meteorological phenomenon, easily explained scientifically, not theologically. A few generations ago, if a loved one got a heart attack, this was a profound theological problem, and we would ask "Why has God done this to us? What have we done wrong?" Sickness was a theological problem. But today we have heart transplants. Heart trouble is no longer a theological problem–it is a transportation problem! How fast can I get to Stanford University and have Dr. Shumway give me a new heart? We no longer need the God of the gaps to explain the blanks in our knowledge. God is dead–because man is alive! That was the ebullient optimism of a decade ago.

But today that unqualified optimism has begun to

fade. The mood of our day is not the same as it was in the 1960s. The 1970s have seen the emergence of a more pessimistic view of man. The space age has not solved the employment problem. The searing agony of over ten years of tragedy in Viet Nam has dashed the heady ebullience which blithely believed that man was the master of all things, and that merely more money could solve all problems.

The full implications of the past half century have come to register with us. We have come to see that side by side with incredible scientific advance there exists another more malignant stream to recent history. The same half century that saw scientific advance has also seen moral decay and the multiplication of human misery. We have seen two great World Wars sandwiched around a depression, followed by two more agonizing conflicts—Korea and Viet Nam—that no one bothered to give a number to. We have even come to question the so-called unbounded goodness of technological advance itself, wondering if it is after all a blessing, or really a curse in disguise. For did not the same technology which produced the 747 also produce the atom bomb which wiped out a million people, and which hovers as a threat over us all today? Did not the same technological advance which produced the heart transplant and the mass-produced automobile also produce pollution and an environmental crisis? Did not the very hunger of the great industrial plants of the western world lead to exploitation of the Third World, and the increasing poverty of the majority of earth's people?

That is the mood of our day, a crisis of confidence, an ebbing of the optimistic view that man is a giant, the master of his own fate. Man instead seems to be ridden, the victim of strange and incomprehensible forces which make mockery of his life, laughing at his advances, and turning those very advances in a grotesquely Mephistophelian manner into the very things which threaten to destroy him. This growing pessimism is perhaps new in theology, but it is not at all new in the larger world outside of theological literature. As one looks back over the most popular writings of the last twenty years one discovers with a near sense of shock that the really thinking writers have come out not with a positive endorsement of the advance of science, but rather a very pessimistic and depressing view of the future of man—there seems to be no hope!

I am not speaking simply of a book such as George Orwell's, *1984*. Here is a book which prophesied years ago that the final result of man's intricate scientific advance could end up a crushing monster choking out freedom. But I am not thinking of books like that. I think instead of books such as those written by Albert Camus and Jean Paul Sartre, French atheistic existentialist writers who won Nobel Prizes for literature. And both men write of the absurdity of life, the apparent inability of man to achieve a wholesome destiny. Sartre writes what begins as a humorous account, and turns into a somber warning. Sartre, nearly blind, tells of how he was walking across the Jardin de Luxembourgh in Paris, and, because he could not see well, he runs into an almond tree. Then comes the humorous part of his story. He asks the chiding question, "Who is running around planting almond trees in my way?" But what begins light heartedly turns into terror. Life is like that! I can never arrive at my goal! I am pushed off my chosen path by unexpected obstacles. I can never achieve my destiny. Life is absurd and there is *No Exit! (No Exit,* of course, is the name of one of his most famous plays).

And Albert Camus, who also won the Nobel Prize for literature, develops the same theme of the inexplicable perversity of the world in which we live. In his great novel *The Plague,* he tells of the doctor who came home to his north African apartment one day and found a dead rat on the doorstep. Same conversation. Who is putting dead rats on my doorstep, forcing me off my chosen path so I have to go around the back way, thrust onto a detour, unable to complete my own desires? And to show how absurd the world is, that dead rat is the carrier of bubonic plague, and the next day half the population of the little African village is destroyed! There is a malignancy in the world cursing and crushing man, the cosmos is absurd, man is unable to achieve his highest goals.

The French atheistic existentialists were not alone in this pessimistic view. Most of the classics of recent American writing breathe out the same odors of despair. Arthur Miller, in *Death of a Salesman,* develops the same attitude of despondency. His hero, or anti-hero, is a bumbling little salesman who never did anything right. Or, more exactly, Willy Loman did do one thing right —he committed suicide. He committed suicide not for negative reasons, but rather so that his sons could get his life insurance money and thus get the decent start in life that Willy never had. But the night before he commits suicide, he forgets to mail in the premium on his policy—and his sons get nothing! And then, as Willy is being buried, one of his sons says plaintively, "Poor Willy, he never knew who he was." Who is Arthur

Miller talking to? Certainly not to a make-believe corpse in a make-believe box on a make-believe stage! He is talking to all of us, giving us his searing negative evaluation of life as he sees it. We are all poor Willies wandering through our maze of electric wires down our corridors of concrete canyons none of us knowing who we are!

Or Holden Caulfield, the hero of a college generation now past. In J. D. Salinger's book, *Catcher in the Rye,* Holden Caulfield is the young lad born with a silver spoon in his mouth, heir of all good fortune, enrolled at the finest preparatory school money can provide. But he finds no meaning there, and he searches elsewhere. He tries to prove his manhood by sleeping with a prostitute, only to find out that animal-like indulgence does not assure maturity. Where then turn? He turns to his English teacher, the one man who had earlier held up light and hope. And, when he is alone with that English teacher, he finds that that teacher is a homosexual trying to bed down with him! Nowhere to turn! And the book closes with young Holden, silver spoon in his mouth, in an insane asylum. Life has no purpose, there are no answers.

That is what contemporary secular literature has been saying. And while those works were being written, so-called theologians were whistling their inane little ditties about God being dead because man was so dramatically alive! The theologians were out of step, a half century too late! They were still captivated by the pre-World War I optimism which once earlier had been fashionable! Before the First World War it may have seemed possible to claim that man every day in every way was getting better all the time! Then, before the First World War, progress seemed to be automatic and advance was inevitable as man climbed ever upward. But that heady optimism was dealt a death blow by the booming cannons of World War I. Man, mighty man, back in the trenches! This was the inconceivable war for the thinking person! This was the war which shattered, for the literary world, the view that man was basically good and getting better. That man could descend into the barbarities of modern warfare massacre was proof for the thinking individual that man's need was greater than a need for education, greater than a need for more time! But the theologians were whistling and telling us that God was not around because man was sufficient unto himself! Thus it was, with no theological answer offered by the church, that the only literature being produced was a literature of despair, the stories of the Holden Caulfields and Willy Lomans, The theologians were out of step, a full step behind, rephrasing the platitudes of the pre-World War I period when the rest of secular literature had gone beyond them!

This, tragically, is usually the case with contemporary theology. Rarely is it a leader, usually it is a follower, always one step behind, always beating the drum for a cause identified by the secular world, but usually beating that drum long after the secular world has moved to new issues.

Look, for example, at the recent theological outburst of literature concerning the civil rights cause. We have perennial sophomores such as Malcolm Boyd, replete with a turtleneck sweater, telling us of the great injustices our black brothers have been exposed to, identifying himself with the fight for black freedom. I have no quarrel with his goal or stated aims. I simply ask him, why was he so late in seeing the issue? He was no prophet, spying out the unrecognized and unheeded injustices of an oppressed people. He was a follower, one step behind. He and all the other theologians who attacked racial injustice did not do so until the black man himself rose up in wrath! Why were there so few theologians writing about racism *before* Martin Luther King? The oppressions were even more real then, before Birmingham! The church is always a step behind in its literature, following rather than leading.

The same comments can be made about ecology. Very fashionable now. Everyone picks up empty beer cans and buys litter bags. Excellent! It is well to seek to preserve our environment and treasure the world we live in as a stewardship given from God. But where were all the theologians *before* Rachel Carson wrote of the threat of a silent spring, a time when man's greed would crush his cosmos? Again the church's writers followed the crowd, identified with that which was then popular, rather than being a step ahead.

And, to return to Revelation, it is precisely that fact which accounts for the renaissance of interest in Revelation today. We live, as we have seen, in a time characterized by a growing pessimism. We live in the middle of a crisis of confidence, a time when man is facing the fact that perhaps he cannot cope with all that surrounds him. This is what lies behind the Age of Aquarius, what rests behind a growing interest in the secular world of things super-celestial. Modern secular man sees mockery being made of his life. His hopes are dashed, his dreams are unfulfilled, and he has come to believe, as it was not possible even a decade ago, in the power of evil. Satan is real today. Far more real than he has been for centuries. He has been restored to life. But not by the theologians! A book by a popular theologian a decade ago about Satan would have rendered that theologian a laughing stock, fair game for a butterfly net! To write in serious theological circles about the devil a decade ago would be to identify yourself with the neanderthal fundamentalist theology of the antedeluvian period! To write about Satan in a learned theological journal was not stylish, and to do so would be to open the door to ridicule. And so nobody did!

But the secular world ventured in where the timidity of the churchmen feared to enter. It was in the secular world that Satan was revived. The secular world returned anew to a belief in evil spirits, sorcery, and seances. At first it was pooh-poohed and lightly dismissed by the sophisticated theologians as merely a recrudesence of drug-infected youthful enthusiasm. But the specter did not go away. *Life* magazine ran a cover story on the rebirth of Satanism; *Time* magazine and *Newsweek* and other respected secular organs began to speak of the reemerging of older beliefs about devils and witches and warlocks and spirits. Suddenly it became fashionable to speak of the devil once more, made fashionable by the secular world.

And once more the theologian, a step behind, began to concentrate on the devil and all his works and all his ways. Now it is fashionable to once more speak of evil celestial powers making mockery of our life, and dashing our hopes, and forcing us into detours, around to the backdoor.

Thus it is that we see a renaissance of literature about Revelation. Here, it appears, is a book which not only takes the reality of the devil seriously, but promises also some future intervention of God when the evil one will be destroyed! What a delightful juxtaposition! On the one hand, we can talk about Satan. On the other hand, we can calm the troubles of our own confused time by telling them that in the future God will act! We may have dead rats on our doorstep now, but Revelation tells us that the end of the world is hastening toward us and what we cannot do for ourselves now God will accomplish for us at the end of time!

Fitting right in with the mood of the moment, the modern theologian can explain Revelation and thus discuss Satan and simultaneously offer future deliverance.

The real tragedy of contemporary study of Revelation is not simply that the theologian is, once more, a step behind, following rather than leading, feeding on current ideas rather than reforming them. The real tragedy is that the mass of modern interpreters have misunderstood the book they are commenting on!

For the simple fact is that Revelation has little to say about Satan, and even less to say about the far future!

If you bought this book expecting to find one more discussion of the end of the world, or the reality of Satan on the present scene, take it back to your bookseller! For this book, like Revelation on which it comments, has not much to say about the end of the world or the current power of the evil one. Instead, it has a great deal to say which runs directly counter to current moods. For the assertion here is that life does have a meaning. We are not to despair or dissolve in a puddle of anxiety which sees sorcerers and witches on all sides. We have no need to peer forward into time to see the hand of God —for the hand of God is present even now, shaping and molding our days.

1

Four Views of Revelation

As we glance down the corridor of centuries of church history, we see that four distinctly different ways of interpreting the book of Revelation have emerged. In this chapter we want to do two things. First, identify and examine those four views. And, second, evaluate those views, indicating which one is the basic point of view of this book.

The "End of History" View

This point of view begins on the assumption that the book of Revelation is concerned with one topic and one topic alone—a discussion of the end of the world! The author, we are told, was transported by the Spirit of God, lifted above the swirling currents of his own day, and allowed to peer into the future seeing all those climactic events which will surround the end of all of human history. In other words, the book has nothing to do with the immediate setting of the author, the problems of the people living in his own day, and no help can be found for understanding its message by examining the circumstances surrounding the time of writing. The book is futuristic, visionary, solely and exclusively concerned with outlining in breathtaking imagery the final events which will mark the end of the world as we know it.

Perhaps the basic thrust of this point of view will become clearer if we move on and describe the second point of view, and then compare and contrast the two.

The "All of History" View

This point of view, like the one we just looked at, agrees that Revelation is describing the end of the world. This view too says that Revelation is futuristic, visionary, concerned with describing that series of cataclysmic events which will mark the end of all of human history. But, this view, unlike the first, goes on from there to argue that Revelation does not describe only the end of the world, but the history of the world from the time of Jesus until the time of his return! In short, we are told that locked up in the pages of this book are the secrets of the ages, told in cryptic form, covering all of the events of history from the days of Jesus' life, death, and resurrection, on down to the end of the days of this planet.

The first view says that Revelation will reveal for us the *final* moments of the *last* days of earth. This view says that careful study of Revelation will yield up *all* the moments of *all the days* of this planet, from the days of Jesus (about A.D. 30) down to the time of his return.

From this point of view, the book of Revelation can

be read like a slide rule. You can figure out, actually calculate, when the end of the world will arrive! You see, if you begin with the assumption that all of human history, from the time of Jesus' first coming down to his second coming, is locked up in its pages, then all you have to do is determine just where you are right now in its pages, and you can calculate exactly when the end will come!

Perhaps an illustration will make this point of view clear. There are 22 chapters in Revelation. And this interpretation believes that all of history, from Jesus' appearance in Galilee down to his appearance in glory at the time of the end, is described within those 22 chapters. That means that chapter 1 can be dated about A.D. 30, the time of Jesus' life, death, and resurrection. And chapter 22 is the date of the end of the world, the year *x*. We do not know—yet—what the date of the year *x* is, that is the unknown that we want to determine, to solve for! And how do we solve for it? Simply by determining where we are right now in the book!

For example, in chapter 16 there are a series of catastrophes which hit the earth, a series of woes afflicting the church. If we can date that series of woes, then we can date the end of the world! Those woes come in chapter 16, about three-fourths of the way through the book. In other words, those woes come about three-fourths of the way between Jesus' first coming and his return! If we can be reasonably positive about when those woes of chapter 16 took place, we can actually calculate the date of the end of the world!

In chapter 16 we read that the world itself seems to go berserk. The powers of darkness seem to prevail. There is no justice in the world. A series of catastrophes break out, the faithful can no longer see the hand of God's justice in human affairs. The devil seems to be in the ascendancy, and right and justice disappear! When could that have been? What is the date of this disappearance of decency? Some could argue that that description fits the time of Hitler, for was that not a time when hell itself belched up its noxious fumes? Six million Jews exterminated in the concentration camps of Dachau, Bergen-Belsen, and Auschwitz! The world embroiled in flames, great stalwarts of God, men like Dietrich Bonhoeffer, were put to death for their confession of God! Does that not fit the atrocities and catastrophes described in chapter 16? And so we decide that it is the age of Hitler, the years surrounding 1940, which is described in chapter 16.

But chapter 16 is three-fourths of the way through the book. That means that the year 1940 is three-fourths of the way through human history, from Jesus' first coming to his second. When, then, will the end of the world come? About the year 2400, for Hitler's years, 1940, make up about three-fourths of 2400! Well, that is not a very satisfactory conclusion for those who look for the end of the world in our time! The end of the world, by that calculation, is still over 500 years away! And so we have to find another date for chapter 16.

How about the time of the Reformation, the time of Martin Luther and the other Reformers? Was not this too a time when the world seemed to have gone berserk? A time when justice had disappeared and the powers of darkness seemed to have taken over? The popes of that time lived in lascivious luxury, positions of power within the church were used for personal pleasure and illegitimate gain! Luther himself, in the heat of Reformation rhetoric, did not even hesitate to call the pope himself the Antichrist, the enemy of God! Would not the time of the Reformation, about 1517, fit the events of chapter 16? If so, look what happens! If chapter 16 is three-fourths of the way through the book, then the age of the Reformation is three-fourths of the way through human history! The year 1517 marks, in a rough way, the three-quarter mark between Jesus' first coming and his return. When will the end of the world come by that reasoning? About the year 1987 or so, in our lifetimes!

That is the way this second point of view, the "All of History" view, approaches the book of Revelation! It assumes that by carefully identifying where we are now in the book, we can calculate the time of the end.

The "Above History" View

This line of interpretation argues that views 1 and 2 above are both mistaken, that Revelation is not concerned with specific moments in history either at the end of time or specific moments in history all through time from Jesus' first coming to his second, but rather that the book is timeless. It is concerned not with specific dates, but rather with general principles. That in the book we find not concrete moments of history described in cryptic fashion, but instead we find a discussion of general themes and enduring concepts which are true of all moments in every age! The struggle between God and the forces of darkness—this, we are told, is not confined to one moment in time, but is true of all time and all places. Certainly we can see in chapter 16 a series of circumstances which seem to describe the age of Hitler. But those circumstances seem to describe equally well the time of the Reformation. And that is the point. The book of Revelation summarizes the struggle not of one period but of all periods! Cannot chapter 16, with its emphasis on the tragedies of the human scene, describe equally well the dark days of the Black Plague in Europe, when three-quarters of England's population was decimated by the bubonic plague? Or cannot that chapter 16 be describing the violent days of persecution back in the early centuries of the church when Diocletian the Roman emperor was trying to snap the spinal column of the church with his vicious persecutions? Or cannot that same chapter be used equally well to describe the trials and tragedies of our own day, when we have had two World Wars squeezed into one generation, sandwiched around a depression, followed up by the demonic fact of drug abuse in our own day? Is there *any* age which is not described in these general words of affliction and woe besieging the human scene?

That is the line of interpretation this third view takes, insisting that we are not to scurry through the pages of Revelation looking for hints and clues which reveal the end of time or specific moments on the way to the end of time, but rather we see in it, in a general and timeless way, the struggles of all ages. Here we see in symbolic form the continuing story, above history, of all ages, all ages locked up in the titanic struggle between the forces of good and the forces of evil. The book is not to be seen, this view argues, as a futuristic or visionary account of the final hours of the planet but rather as an outline of the struggles of all the saints, and the story of God's identification with the church in its trials of every age.

The "In That History" View

This fourth avenue of approach is distinctly different from the three we have already looked at. This view claims that the book of Revelation is neither visionary, concerned only about the end of time, nor is it timeless, summarizing principles which are always true. Instead, this view argues that the book of Revelation was written for the people who first read it. It was aimed at a people who lived about 2,000 years ago, living in western Turkey, near to the island of Patmos where the author was imprisoned, and that its primary meaning was addressed to their problems, their needs, their circumstances! The book had an immediate audience, a specific purpose, and that purpose is locked up in the history of that time.

If you want to understand the true meaning of the book, therefore, you must begin with the history of that time. You must know the situation of the writer, the problems of the people to whom he was writing. You must know what the author was trying to tell the people right then and there. Certainly the book has meaning to those of us who read it later. We can still profit from reading it even though our circumstances are different from those of the people who first read it. But, if you want to truly understand what the book says *to us,* you must first of all know what it said *to them,* to the people to whom it was originally addressed!

The book, from this line of interpretation, is not speculative stargazing, trying to peer ahead into the mists of time to unravel far future events, nor is it an abstract discussion of timeless truths seen in every age, but it is a specific message to a concrete time and place, addressed to an actual people troubled by immediate and overwhelming problems, and the first task of the interpreter is to determine the meaning and the message the book held for the people then alive in *that* time!

We have now looked at the four broad ways in which the book of Revelation has been interpreted. We now try to evaluate those four views, and indicate which of the four is the basic view of this book.

The first thing to be said is this: there is probably an element of truth in all of these points of view—except the second.

Take the first point of view for example, the futuristic or "end of history" view. Certainly the confessing Christian must insist that God's Word is concerned about the time of the end, the return of Jesus ushering to a close all of human history as we know it. This confession, that Christ will return, is absolutely basic to the Christian church. We know that one of the dearest dogmas of the earliest Christian church was their hope, their absolutely unwavering certainty, that Jesus Christ was coming, and that right soon!

One of the first and most famous prayers of the church was the one word cry, "Maranatha," an Aramaic word which meant "O Lord, come!" The church was convinced of the certainty of Jesus' return, that he would come back and rescue his beleaguered saints. Even as he had conquered the grave and risen from the dead, in the same manner he would overcome the tragedies of sin, death, and the devil for those who called on his holy name. This belief in a real end of the world was for them a true and abiding hope, and it remains the same for the church today.

Christ is coming, we confess, every time we say the

words of the Apostles' Creed. Every time we utter those phrases ". . . from thence he shall come to judge the quick and the dead. . . . I believe in . . . the resurrection of the body, and the life everlasting" we are making our eschatological confession, voicing our conviction that the end of the world and the return of Jesus are unshakeable truths to which we cling. So, the point of view which sees in the writings of Scripture a forward look to the return of Jesus is a legitimate point of view. More than legitimate, it is one of the cornerstones or underpinnings of our faith. It is our affirmation that this world is not the whole show, that man has an eternal destiny, and that at the end of our days is our gracious God who gathers us unto himself.

And the third point of view, the one which argues that on the pages of Revelation we see certain timeless truths which are true and valid for all times and all places, that too is a legitimate line of interpretation. Certainly if God's Word is relevant and vital for all men, it must speak to all men. The message cannot be simply, on the one hand, for men who lived long ago, nor reserved exclusively for yet unborn generations. The Word of God, to be the Word of God, cannot be solely an archaic museum piece telling us solely what people long ago used to believe. Nor can it be solely and exclusively a future forecast of what men later on will see. It must speak to us, right here, right now! There is a timeless character to God's relevation which allows us, which allows the men of the Middle Ages, and which allows the men of the first age and the last age of the church all to gather together and hear the counsel of God!

But the second view, the argument that says that if we find the clues we can decipher the future and identify the date of the end of the world, that point of view must be repudiated entirely. It is blasphemous, presumptuous, and unscriptural! It flies into the very face of Scripture itself. Paul, quoting the words of Jesus, insists that the time of the end is unknown to us all: "But as to the times and seasons, brethren, you have no need to have anything written to you. For you yourselves know well that the day of our Lord will come like a thief in the night" (1 Thess. 5:1-2). Like a thief in the night! Its hour of arrival unknown. The exact moment of its coming not to be deciphered. Jesus himself insists that not even he, not even the Son of God himself, knows when that final hour will come. That is a mystery known to God and to God alone! "But of that day or that hour no one knows, not even the angels in heaven, nor the Son, but only the Father" (Mark 13:32). Those who with their pious charts and their pontificating predictions treat the book of Revelation like a celestial slide rule revealing the date and the hour of the end of time are blasphemous. They claim more knowledge than Jesus himself. There is no legitimacy, no Bible base, for this line of interpretation.

But, unfortunately, this avenue of approach is the most popular today! This second view, which eyes the book of Revelation as if it were some cosmic calendar giving us the clues to the culmination of all of human history is the most widespread, well known, and often endorsed attitude toward Revelation today. Every wildeyed sectarian who has ever examined the book of Revelation treats it as if it will yield up the date of the final hour.

Using the slide rule approach, Judge Russell, the founder of the Jehovah's Witnesses sect, predicted when the end of the world would arrive. This same approach leads the sectarians of our day to trumpet to all who will hear that the signs are being fulfilled and that we can see, if we have eyes to see, that we are engulfed in the final hours and all of human history is hastening to its close. Indeed, this avenue of interpretation is so widely endorsed today that there are many who have been deluded into thinking not only that it is a legitimate line of interpretation, but that it is the *only* line of interpreation! There are those who unthinkingly and naively have fallen victim to these shrill sectarian voices and—never having been exposed to an alternate interpretation—just take for granted, no matter how uncomfortable such a view might make them, that this is indeed the basic thrust of Revelation, to prepare us for the final hours and reveal to us when that final hour will come.

Nonsense! The book of Revelation is *not* a timetable, to be read like an airline schedule, telling us when we can expect the final end to arrive.

How, then, *are* we to understand this strange and mysterious book? The main line of traditional conservative Christianity has always emphasized the *fourth* point of view. And that is the interpretation *this* book will endorse! What did the book mean to the people who first read it? What message was meant to the first readers? What were the setting of the author, the problems of the people then, the afflictions and trials of the first readers? *Those* are the essential questions. If we cannot understand *those* issues, the book of Revelation will remain forever a closed book to us, revealing up none of its truths.

Certainly, as we have already said, there is a futuristic thrust to the book as the author and the audience peer ahead to the close of the age. And certainly, as we have said, there is a timeless quality to the book which transcends the immediate struggle of that past day. But those emphases and ideas are not the primary point of the book. This book, like all the books of the New Testament, was not written in a vacuum, independent of the circumstances of the writer and readers. *All* of the books of the New Testament find their first and most significant meaning in the lives of the first people to read them. Any approach to any of the New Testament books which does not recognize that fact will simply be totally incapable of comprehending the New Testament!

For example, why did Paul write the letter to the Galatians? Every serious scholar of the New Testament gives you one specific answer to that question. Paul had baptized the Galatians, who were Gentiles, and had called them Christians without laying on them the burden of the Jewish law. And that act was opposed by a band of Christian Jews who insisted that one could not be saved by faith in Jesus alone, but rather that faith in Jesus had to be supplemented by the Jewish law. And Galatians is Paul's response to that attack of these Jewish Christians. He thunders through those pages that faith in Jesus is sufficient unto salvation—man does not need the works of the law to earn the favor of God.

Now certainly there is a timeless quality to that message! Surely there is a sense in which the conclusions of Paul, addressed to the Galatians, tells us something today too. That proclamation of Paul has not been outdated by the passage of time, but still today summarizes God's dealings with men. But the timelessness of the message must not be allowed to obscure the central fact that it is only the circumstances of that specific struggle of Paul in that time which pour meaning and content into the message. If we do not understand what the letter meant to the people who first read it, we really cannot understand what the letter means today either.

The same kind of case can be made for 1 Corinthians. The church in Corinth was fragmented, divided, a warring group of cliques and factions. And to them Paul speaks of what the church ought to be, not divided but united as the body of Christ.

Surely this insight of Paul, that the church ought to be an organic whole, each part serving the entire body, tells us something today too! But the timeless element of the message can be grasped only when we first see what the original circumstances of the Corinthians were and what Paul was seeking to say to them in their time!

All of the New Testament books must be seen in this way. They are not cosmic stones which fell fully written from heaven, independent of the circumstances of their first readers. On the contrary, these books grew up out of concrete difficulties of specific peoples in given places in space and time. Thus if any of those books is to yield up its full message, the first thing the investigator has to study is the meaning of the book to the people who first read it.

What good would it have done to the first readers of the book of Revelation to learn that the end of the world would come about the year 2457? How would that comfort them? How would that hold up their hand during persecution in their own day? Such a line of interpretation fails to recognize the original setting of the first audience, the meaning the book had for its first readers. And that line of interpretation we reject entirely here. The book of Revelation does speak of the end, and it does have timeless truths in it. But those are secondary things. The primary task is to ask ourselves, "What did the book mean to the people who lived in western Turkey 2,000 years ago?" That question must be answered first of all, or the book remains an obscure riddle.

2

Revelation—What the Word Means

In the previous chapter we rejected the view that looks at Revelation as if it were a timetable of far future events. But the question has to be asked, "Where did that view come from? How did it get started?" And the answer is found at least in part in the title. The very word "Revelation" carries overtones of prediction, conjures up images of supernatural disclosure of celestial comings, suggests clairvoyance or futuristic visions.

But in Greek, the original language of the book, the title is *apocalypse*. And that word, *apocalypse,* means something entirely different to the New Testament scholar. The word *apocalypse* refers to a specific kind of writing, a given class of literature which flourished at a specific period of Jewish history. Apocalyptic literature describes a type of writing with definite characteristics, concrete purposes, identifying marks. Our first task, if we truly want to understand Revelation, is to recognize that it does not stand alone. There are *many* apocalyptic books! *The Testament of the Twelve Patri-*

archs, The Book of Jubilees, The Assumption of Moses, The Similitudes of Enoch, are but a few of the many books we call apocalyptic literature, a type of literature which flourished at a specific time of Jewish history, written in a peculiar way with identifiable goals. And the book of Revelation bears most of the marks of apocalyptic literature. Thus, if we want to understand the book, we had first of all better understand apocalyptic literature, and the apocalyptic period which produced it.

The story begins about three and a half centuries before Jesus was born. A young Greek warrior, barely able to shave, strapped on a sword and went to war. At eighteen years of age, he led his armies out of the Macedonian mountains, swept across the Hellespont into Asia, shattered the Persian fleet at the Battle of Issus in 333 B.C., destroyed the Asian hordes, and pushed the pendulum of power from Asia into Europe. The battles he fought were of such heroic stature that the world ever since has added the words "the great" to his name, Alexander the Great!

But the very drama and magnitude of Alexander's heroic military feats only serve to obscure the real character of the man. For Alexander was not primarily a soldier. No man does the things he did out of a lust for power alone. No man accomplishes the incredible as he did driven merely by negative military ambition. Alexander was not primarily a soldier; he was an evangelist! An evangelist for man! He was convinced of the power of man, driven by the desire to share his enormous view of man as an exalted figure able to change the world, harness his own destiny, mold his own future. He believed that man was a giant—and that was the dream he wanted to spread around the world.

Perhaps that dream of the Greek warrior can best be seen by remembering a story told about him and his teacher. Behind every great man there is a great–teacher! And Alexander had a great teacher, Aristotle. The story is that one day when Alexander was a youth, he was sitting with his teacher Aristotle in a lonely cave in northern Greece doing his school work, the lad poring over his studies, his teacher musing nearby, brewing a pot of tea over a small fire in the cave. And as Aristotle abstractedly watched the water boil, he saw the bubbling water give off a vapor which rose and, when it hit the cool upper walls of the cave, condense as droplets of water. And then he cried out, the story goes, "Eureka, Alexander, we have found it!" Found what? The secret of rainfall! That's the way it is in the wide world of nature! The sun acts like the fire causing the water vapor to rise up off the streams and lakes, and when it rises up it hits the cool atmosphere above and condenses into droplets and falls like rain! Alexander, we have found the secret of rainfall! Alexander, we can make the deserts bloom! Alexander, man has no longer to live hemmed in by narrow river bottoms or fertile fields! Now we can produce rain! Now we can change our environment, change the world, make arid areas grow, and control our own destiny! It might take awhile to learn how to make fires that big–but that is only a technical problem. Now we know the *principle,* the *secret* of rainfall, and knowing that we can alter the world and shape our own fortunes, no longer dependent on the whims of nature!

That was the spirit Alexander breathed in from his teacher. The conviction that man was a giant, ruler of his own world, shaper of his own future, master of his own destiny! This heroic concept of man as a giant dominated Alexander, and indeed through him dominated the entire Greek world. A worship of man, man the magnificent! It shows up in ancient Greek sculpture. Always the figures are larger than life, revealing man as huge, as powerful!

This is the dream which carried Alexander to the ends of the earth. His evangelism. His certitude of the sovereignty of man. He wanted to share this magnificent vision of the power of man. And that is why, when his armies rolled, they were symbolized not only by the soldier's sword but by the librarian's card as well! Wherever Alexander went the scientists were soon to follow. In North Africa, he founded the famous city named after himself, Alexandria. And Alexandria had the world's largest library! It was to share the vision of mighty man that the armies rolled out of Macedonia and brought Greece to the crest of empire's glory, ruling over three continents!

But, to move ahead, Alexander died at an early age, barely 30 years old. However, when he died his dreams of mighty man did not perish with him. Those dreams were passed on to the generals who took his empire, divided it up, and ruled on after him. Those first generals became kings, and established dynasties which continued to rule the world for centuries after his passing. In the Middle East, just north of what we now call the Holy Land, the rule and the reign went to a line of kings, descendants of Alexander's general, who called themselves Antiochus. Antiochus I, Antiochus II, Antiochus III, Antiochus IV. But, when we get to Antiochus IV, about the year 170 B.C., we find a man who wanted to be more than a number. He wanted to be a name.

And so Antiochus IV stops calling himself Antiochus IV and calls himself instead Antiochus Epiphanes—destined to be one of the blackest names in all of Jewish history!

The name itself which he took, Epiphanes, tells you something of the dreams and grandiose schemes of this man. Epiphanes comes from two Greek words, *epi* and *phanos*. The light, the light shining through—that is what the word means.

That is what Antiochus IV called himself, "I am Epiphanes, the light of the world!" He wanted to share the insights of Alexander. He also wanted to be an evangelist, to preach the glories of man.

But to whom was he to preach this good news? With whom was he to share the glories of man the giant? Over which people did he rule? The Jews! That is where his kingdom was, in the land of the Jews. And so he tried to evangelize the Jews, share with them his visions of man's power. But the Jews were not interested. They had their own views! They exalted not man but God. For them, the center of the universe was not mighty man but God who had spoken the word and all things came forth. It was God who ruled the cosmos, held the mountains in his hand, and cradled the seas. The earth was the Lord's and the fulness thereof. Man was not to be adored, but the God of Abraham, Isaac, and Jacob. And thus the Jews resisted.

And when the Jews resisted, Antiochus Epiphanes struck back with a frenetic fury that took one's breath away! He would force the Jews to accept his ways! He saw that before he could plant he had to plow. Before he could sow the seeds of man's glory, he had to rip up the religion of the Jews. Antiochus Epiphanes unleashed the most devastating persecution the Jews had ever known. They had seen trouble before. They had been born, as a nation, in the iron furnace of Egypt. They had passed under the sword of the Assyrians, their homeland had been ravaged by the Babylonians, they had been enslaved for centuries under the Persians. But never before had they passed through a night of horror like the one Antiochus Epiphanes dealt them! All the energies of this demented man were focused on one goal —the total destruction of the Jewish religion.

The first thing he did was to proscribe the reading of the Mosaic law. Anyone found reading the sacred books would be executed. He defiled the Jewish temple. The strict Jew, to this very day, looks on the pig as unclean. Antiochus took a whole herd of pigs into the temple and slaughtered them there, defiling the altar, letting their unclean blood roll across the sacred place!

But the defiling of the temple was only the beginning, not the end, of Antiochus' wild schemes. Every Jewish boy, on the eighth day of his life, was supposed to be circumcised according to the law of Moses. Said Antiochus, if any Jewish boy is circumcised, that boy will be immediately put to death. The priest who performed the ritual would be slain instantly. The father of the dead child would be executed. And the body of the dead baby would be fastened around the neck of the mother, and there it would rot, carrying away the mother in the putrefying stench of the decaying corpse of her own child. A night of darkness descended on the Jews, a period of persecution unparalleled in their sorry history of woe and suffering.

Out of this maelstrom of malignant woe all the sects of the Jews, as we meet them on the pages of the New Testament, emerged. What did the Jews do in the face of these persecutions? What would *any* people do? They began to fragment. Some capitulated, gave in, went along with the ways of Antiochus, took up Greek thought patterns. Others fought back, resisted, heroically took a stand no matter what the cost.

Most of us know of the Maccabees, that little band of brothers inspired by the example of their father who fought back, who resisted, and who miraculously won, in 143 B.C. a temporary but lustrous freedom from Greek domination. But the Maccabees were not the only party or sect to spring up out of the chaos of Antiochus' persecution. All the parties of Jesus' time find their beginnings here.

For example, the Sadducees find their historical beginnings in this period under Antiochus Epiphanes. The Sadducees were the "Greek" Jews, the compromisers, the ones who abandoned the faith of their fathers in order to avoid persecution. This is why, eventually, the Sadducees rose to positions of power and prominence in New Testament times. The Greek rulers, and the Romans after them, propelled the Sadducees forward because they discovered that the Sadducees were pliable, willing to compromise their convictions, and thus could be used, if they were given important posts, to help control the Jews.

The Pharisees too find their historical beginnings in the period of persecution under Antiochus Epiphanes. These were the "Jewish" Jews, the ones who would not compromise Jewish ways, who resisted Greek ways. Some of them later became proud and hypocritical and were denounced by Jesus himself for their false piety, but what a few later became must not obscure what the Pharisees meant during the dark days of persecution. They were at one time the noblest element of all of Judaism, willing to die rather than compromise Jewish religion.

There is yet another group born out of this hour of agony, a group little known until our own day, just now beginning to receive the recognition their movement deserves. We are speaking of the Essenes, the group that lived near the Dead Sea, whose writings, recently discovered, are called the Dead Sea Scrolls. The Sadducees gave up, yielded, compromised their faith. The Pharisees fought back, stayed on the scene, and resisted. But the Essenes withdrew, gave up on the world, abandoned life in this world, and secluded themselves at the Dead Sea, the most barren hostile place on all the face of the world. The Dead Sea is the lowest place on the globe, arid, sterile, forbidding. Nothing grows there, a viciously hostile deceptive mockery of the earth's supposed goodness.

And there the Essenes went to live. Even more incredibly, in the entire Dead Sea basin, there is one green and fertile place, the northeastern corner of the sea where the Jordan river dumps in its fresh water. There things grow, there things are green. But the Essenes went to live on the opposite side of the sea! At the foot of the Judean hills they settled down, and those Judean hills acted like a reflector, multiplying the heat of the noonday, crushing men with its lethal rays. And there, in the most forsaken corner of that forsaken land, the Essenes settled and established their little community called Qumran.

Why such a desolate corner? Because they were convinced, as incredible as it might sound to modern scientific man, that this world had fallen prey to Satan and was under the direct control of the devil! That is why they abandoned the world, and found its most vicious corner in which to live. They wanted nothing to do with the pleasures of this world. All the pleasures of this world were demonic, deceptive, determined by the devil. They gave up marriage, that we know. If a husband and a wife joined the community, never again would they see each other. Husband would live in one area, wife in another. No marriage, no sex. Why procreate and bring more children into a world ruled by the devil? Barely any food at all, no private property, they shared in common the little they had, eating all their meals together, meager as those meals were. Why feast the body and indulge the appetite when all the things of this world were ruled by Satan?

The persecutions under Epiphanes convinced them that this world was no longer God's place but Satan's realm. How account for the fact that a man who tried to live by the law and have his son circumcised could be slain? Surely that was not the will of a loving God. It must be the work of God-opposing forces, it must be the activity of Satan! That is the basic conviction of the Essenes, and that is why they fled to such a hostile area, for they would have nothing to do with a world ruled by the devil!

After this extended discussion, we can consider the apocalyptic period and the nature of apocalyptic literature. What we have just seen about the Essenes—their conviction that the world was somehow sundered from God and ruled over by Satan—*that* is the basic starting point of apocalyptic literature. Again and again, running through all of the books we earlier mentioned as making up apocalyptic literature, we see the stress on the awesome might of Satan. All of this literature concentrates on his fall.

Earlier, in Jewish thought, Satan was seen as a servant of God, one of the heavenly court, waiting on the Father, doing his will. But one of the dominant themes of apocalyptic literature is the insistence that there was a revolt in heaven when Satan ceased being a servant and became an enemy. No longer concerned with executing the will of God, he exercised his own malignant malevolent desire. The Book of Enoch has two separate accounts of the fall of the angels. The Book of Jubilees has its own account. In all apocalyptic literature the evil nature of Satan is expounded. He is no longer the servant of God but an enemy. And since he has seized power in the world, the world itself takes on a perverted strain. It is for this reason that Antiochus can exercise such awesome evil. For there stands behind him the celestial evil influence of Satan himself. Surely the tragedy of persecution could not be traced back to God. Out of the crucible of persecution arose the conviction that the world was separated from God, and had now become a battlefield where Satan exercised power.

That is the first "mark" or characteristic of apocalyptic literature. It is pessimistic literature. In one sense, it is literature of despair. It is written during a time of persecution. It recognizes the activity not only of God but of Satan. It assumes the actors on the human scene are celestial evil powers, breathing fury into human tyrants like Antiochus, making mockery of the goodness of life that God had intended.

But apocalyptic literature only *begins* here. It does not finish on this note of despair. In the deepest sense, apocalyptic literature is a positive affirmation that God will have the last word, that God will destroy the devil and all his works and all his ways. The apocalyptic writers were convinced to the depth of their being that God would bring forth the victory, that his rule would once more be established. In the deepest sense, apocalyptic literature is not at all a literature of despair, but is a message of hope and comfort and assurance. It is the shout of faith, the affirmation of conviction, the assurance that God will prevail. For example, one of the most famous scrolls found at the Dead Sea is called *The War of the Sons of Light and the Sons of Darkness.* And in that scroll we read of the hope of the Essenes. Yes, the world is now under the powers of darkness, but there will come a future invasion by God, the destruction of the powers of darkness, the re-establishment of God's rule. His kingdom will come! His will will be done on earth as it is in heaven. The time is coming when God will rescue his people and crush the tyrants who persecute them! Apocalyptic literature, then, has this as its second "mark" or characteristic—the promise that the persecuting forces will be destroyed, and God's people will win out.

The third and fourth characteristics of apocalyptic literature belong together. First, the literature was always written in disguised or cryptic or symbolic language. Its meaning was not literal but hidden. And, second, it was pesudonymous, that is, it was not written under the author's real name. Instead, it was given a fictitious author, usually a name out of the distant past.

Now the reasons for these two characteristics are self-evident, in the light of the historical setting. Remember, when these writings were being produced, a persection was taking place, the people were immediately and murderously exposed to the activity of enemies. What would have happened to any author who wrote clearly, not in disguised words, and who signed his own name? What would have happened to an author who would have explicitly said, "Antiochus is an instrument of the devil himself and God will destroy him, and my name is Joshua Ben Sira and I live in the northeast corner of Jerusalem?" The answer is obvious! In the first place, the author would be killed, and, second, the writing would be suppressed!

Therefore apocalyptic writing developed the way it did, written in camouflaged or concealed language, and then circulated under a name of a figure of long ago. Substitutes had to be found, artificial images had to be employed. Antiochus' name had to be replaced by some other name, some other figure. And older, now no longer living persons, had to be passed off as authors. And the Jews found a way to get past the censors. They talked, in the apocalyptic literature, not of Antiochus Epiphanes, but of Nebuchadnezzar of Babylon of centuries earlier, or they wrote of cosmic beings, devils and demons, flirting on the fringes of heaven. And they signed the writings by ascribing them to worthies of the Jewish past!

That is why the apocalyptic literature bears such names as *The Testament of the Twelve Patriarchs.* The twelve patriarchs were the twelve sons of Jacob, the founders of the twelve tribes of Israel, dead centuries ago. That is why they called it the *Book of Enoch,* for Enoch was the third generation of mankind, following Adam and Eve and Cain and Abel! Enoch was long dead and could not be persecuted by Antiochus. The Jews who read this literature clearly understood what was being said. They saw through the symbolism and the disguised imagery and the artificial authors. They knew the literature was not ancient, actually written by the twelve sons of Israel or the departed Enoch. And they understood that the real villain was not truly Nebuchadnezzar of centuries ago. They clearly grasped the underlying message of comfort and hope. They saw that what was really being said, beyond the imaginary imagery, was the promise that Antiochus would be destroyed!

But the Greeks, the persecutors, did not grasp the immediate meaning of the literature! They thought it was but musty musings of a long past age. They allowed it to circulate, taking it at face value, assuming that this was but an ancient writing unrelated to the present! They failed to see, because it was written about figures no longer alive and apparently produced centuries ago by men long dead, that this was an exhortation to hold on, a plea to endure, a promise that God would vindicate his holiness and destroy his immediate enemies and liberate his people. The Greeks failed to see that the language was symbolic and non-literal, that the authorship was fictitious, and that in reality this was not ancient history but present theology written for a specific purpose. A purpose of comfort to beleaguered saints, a promise of victory to persecuted people!

This is the way the Book of Daniel must be understood. The Book of Daniel has twelve chapters, dividing themselves down the middle. The first six chapters describe the exile, the persecution under Babylon from 586 B.C. to 536 B.C. when the Jews were ripped out of their homeland and carried off into slavery. In those six chapters we read of the attempt of Nebuchadnezzar of Babylon to break the spinal column of the Jews, his attempt to wrench them loose from their religion. And we read of the heroic stands of those who resisted. We read of Shadrach, Meshach, and Abednego who were willing to die rather than compromise their faith, and of how they were cast into the fiery furnace. But we also read of how God delivered them. In the furnace were *four* figures, not three! The angel of God was present with them, protecting them from harm. They should die, yet they would live, thanks to the protection of God. We read of Daniel who would not bend the knee to a foreign God, and how he too was condemned to die, thrown into the lion's den. But God delivered him too. God was an everpresent help in the time of trouble. Those who resisted would be delivered. That is the theme or tempo of the first six chapters of the book.

But then in the second half, the writing becomes increasingly obscure, camouflaged, incomprehensible to all but those who have the eyes to see. The vision moves away from the time of the exile and looks forward to the "end of time" or the "time of the end." As visions of final apocalyptic victory are painted, we are told how in the latter days God's power would be seen once more, and even as Daniel was earlier delivered, so also in the final days of the end the people of God would be delivered. There emerges a promise of hope, an assurance of final victory in later persecutions. The book can well be summarized in the words of the famous hymn, "O God our help in ages past, our hope for years to come."

For centuries of Christian history, the Book of Daniel was taken in a literalistic way, as if it were actually written by Daniel himself during the time portrayed, the time of the exile of Babylon, 586 B.C. It was simply assumed that in the final chapters Daniel was lifted up in an ecstatic trance and allowed to peer into the distant future and given the details surrounding the end of the world. The book was seen in a visionary futuristic predictive way, as if the author was outlining far distant days not his own.

But now we have come to see that Daniel is an apocalyptic book, written not during the exile but written during the time of Antiochus Epiphanes. It is apocalyptic. It is written in deliberately obscure language, and it is passed off under a fictitious name, and it is intended to give an immediate message of comfort to persecuted people pounded from pillar to post by Antiochus. The book is not idle speculative stargazing written by a man in a trance lifted up out of his own time to give coy hints of final times. It is written by a man desperately seeking to encourage his own people, and the only way he can do it is by resorting to symbolism and pseudonymity. He is crying out to those who have eyes to see, that just as God protected Daniel in the days of Nebuchadnezzar so also God will protect the loyal during these final days, during those critical hours of persecution under Antiochus. Hold firm! Stand fast! God helped Shadrach, Meshach, and Abednego, and in precisely that same way his power shall be seen in the lives, right now, of all those who do not buckle and bow down and worship the false gods of Antiochus.

Any attempt to see Daniel as purely visionary, telling us in disguised language just exactly when the end will come and at what moment human history will come to a close, is not only mistaken; it is blasphemous and presumptuous. It assumes more knowledge about identifying the time of the end of the world than even Jesus would claim. Any attempt to see in the cryptic language of Daniel the signs of our own times or of the literal end of history is an attempt based on ignorance of what apocalyptic literature was and what it was trying to do! Those who see in God and Magog contemporary evidences of the rise of Russia and Red China have not read Daniel right—they have instead given free reign to their own imaginations! Such interpretations are the fantasies of men who do not know how to read apocalyptic literature.

Certainly it is true that God indeed could lift up a man and reveal to him the secrets of the far distant future and give us relief maps of 20th century political science if he so wished! But *would* he? *That* is the question! And the testimony of all of the rest of Scripture is that he would not! God does not ignore one generation in order to reveal exotic secrets to yet unborn peoples. God meets his people where they are, in their need. And God speaks to their immediate problems, offering them solace and hope in dark hours of storms. And *that* is the way Daniel must be seen! It is a message of hope, written during the apocalyptic period, to people being persecuted, assuring them that they are not abandoned, but that just as God was with Daniel so also he is with them in that dire hour. Stand firm, do not be like the Sadducees, be willing to die even as the Pharisees were willing to die, and God will deliver you; the sons of darkness will be overcome by the sons of light!

Several more points must be made before we can conclude this discussion. Remember, the apocalyptic writers, in order to get past the censors, must deliberately camouflage their writings. They cannot describe things in a literal, obvious fashion or else their persecutors will see what is actually being said and the books will be confiscated and burned, and the message of hope will not be heard. Thus they must use cryptic symbols, disguise their language, hide their true meaning in order to get past the censors. And the problem is that they succeeded!

If they got past the censors, because the censors did not know all of contemporary Jewish culture, they also get past us, because for us too some of the keys are lost! We can understand much of the symbolism of a Book of Daniel because some of the symbolism is so obvious. When Daniel talks about Nebuchadnezzar we can easily see that he means Antiochus Epiphanes. But other symbols are not so obvious. Just as the Jewish writer was able to confuse the censors and get by them, so also they get by us.

And what is the greatest danger, the greatest temptation, when we do not correctly understand the true meaning of an author? Why, to insert our own meaning of course! And that is what takes place with all too much present-day interpretation of the Book of Daniel! We are no longer always entirely sure what the author meant, what he was alluding to, what meaning rested behind his imagery, and so we end up substituting our own imagery and calling it his meaning. That is why we have so many wild interpretations of this book on all sides of us today.

And what has been said about Daniel is true also of the book of Revelation. Revelation is apocalyptic literature. It too is written during a time of persecution. It too is a message of hope to an immediate troubled people. And it too is written in purposely disguised language, designed to get past the censor. And it too is successful. That is, Revelation too has some cryptic symbolism and obscure language the keys for which are lost. And as a result, because we cannot always be positive of exactly what the author of Revelation is saying, the temptation is always there to read in our own exotic interpretations, substituting our own bizarre imaginings and predictions in place of the concrete solid message of comfort the author meant his book to be.

Anyone who approaches the book of Revelation and finds in it far-flung predictions of a future scene, unraveling for us all the mysteries of the closing moments, is a person who has failed to understand the true nature of apocalyptic, who has fallen victim to the temptation to insert his own meanings into the obscure references of an author who deliberately sought to disguise his language so it could elude the censors.

We will never be able to be absolutely positive of the specific meaning of each verse of Revelation. We will never be 100 percent certain of exactly what hidden meaning lies behind this specific imagery or that specific verse. We will never have that absolute certainty simply because the author was successful! He disguised his language. But because we can never have that certainty, we must be especially careful not to insert our own pet theories or ideas, nor to ignore the primary and obvious thrust of the book, namely, to assure a specific people in an immediate hour that God was with them. It was a promise of deliverance aimed at a given moment in time. It was written to speak to the problem of suffering and persecution that the early church was undergoing, and if we want to meet the meaning of the book we have to approach it from that point of view. What was the problem of those people in that history? What were the circumstances of the readers and of the author? What was he trying to say in his deliberately disguised language?

3

John, Domitian, and Patmos

Rome ruled the world. In the days of John the Apostle, the great gray eagles of the Roman legions were unfurled across three continents. From the fog-shrouded, sheep-covered moorlands of north England, on through sunny Segovia in Spain, the sandy beaches of north Africa, to the fabled cities of the Orient, Rome ruled the world.

This vast empire had not been easily won, nor was it easily maintained. The heavy hand of Caesar reached into the destinies of captive, subject peoples from one end of the Mediterranean to the other. And people then as now yearned for freedom, for independence, for the right of self-determination. There was no natural or innate loyalty to Rome. The empire had been carved out by the sword, and it was military power alone which insured its survival.

To that the Romans addressed themselves. The Romans were shrewd and cunning administrators of their conquered colonies. They knew very well that military dominance alone could not assure survival of their sweeping domain, for the sword could only unify men's bodies, not weld together their spirits. Some way had to be found not only of making men subject to Rome, but of making them loyal to Rome. Or else the crest of empire's glory would ebb. And the shrewd and cunning Romans found what they thought would be a way to do that welding.

Under the aegis of Roman power there lived men of many languages, of every color skin. And the Romans clearly saw that the only way that enduring loyalty to Rome could be achieved was to make all men brothers. But men cannot be brothers unless they have a common father. It is religion, not the sword, that ties humanity together. It is only when men have God as their father that they can be brothers.

And thus the Romans invented a new religion, a religion of the state, a religion in which the Caesar would be the god. Loyalty to Rome could be won by giving the emperor the status of a god, and attaching to the throne the reverential awe of worship! Unity could be achieved by casting over the crown the devotion due to deity. These many men of every color skin could be made brothers if they all together adored the Roman Caesar as their father and their god.

The man who spun off this dream of divinity was Domitian, Roman emperor from A.D. 81 to 96. To this very day in western Asia Minor, in the ruins of ancient Ephesus in modern day Turkey, one can still see the remains of the temple of Domitian, the place where all the emperor's subjects could—and must—worship him. The temple built, a decree went out from Domitian that all men were to come and worship the Roman emperor. There in the temple burned an eternal flame, and all the subjects of Roman power were to come and cast a pinch of incense on the altar, paying homage unto the Caesar as their god. It was a shrewd and cunning move. In the relaxed and casual religious attitude of yesteryear, there were few who would resist. Another god, one more or less, made little difference, and most were willing to worship in this way as they were ordered to do. And in the act of worshipping Caesar the bonds of brotherhood were supposedly to be knit. Here, in the common shared act of worship, brotherhood would be achieved. Rome would win not only the begrudging and servile obedience of the subjects, but their religious devotion!

And living in Ephesus in the days of Domitian was the aged apostle John, son of Zebedee, brother of James, disciple of Jesus, a man whose whole adult life had been spent in adoring Jesus as Savior and Lord. He was not about to bend the knee, in old age, after many years of consecration unto Christ, to a mere mortal, a human usurper, a Roman emperor. He, and most of his followers, refused to cast the pinch of incense on the altar of Domitian. And a persecution broke out.

The Romans could have killed him on the spot. But the Romans were shrewd and cunning colonial administrators. And they knew that if they killed John they would be giving to the new upstart religion of Christianity a martyr. Nothing renews the spirit of a minority movement more than having a martyr. And the Romans knew that, and they were not about to give the Christians the martyr that would cause their movement to grow. Thus the Romans, instead of killing the old man for his refusal to worship Domitian, instead picked him up and carried him off prisoner to the Roman prison island lying off the Ephesian coast, the island of Patmos.

There on Patmos, in a Roman prison, John wants to write a letter of comfort and assurance, a letter of encouragement and exhortation, to his persecuted fellow Christians back on the mainland. The people back home are discouraged, on the brink of despair, ready to give up the faith. The imprisonment of their apostle is more than a human tragedy. It is a theological dilemma, a contradiction of all they believed.

The first Christian confession of faith was but a three-word proclamation, "Jesus is Lord!" That first Christian creed can be found in the pages of the New Testament itself, and in it was summarized the essence of all of early Christian conviction—that Jesus truly was Lord. That Jesus truly was the most powerful figure to ever enter into human history! Here was the confession which proclaimed to the world that Jesus was the Son of God, ruler of heaven and earth, vanquisher of sin, death, and the devil! That was their confession.

But what was the fact? Where were the evidences of Jesus' supposed superiority? Was Jesus truly Lord? If so, why was he unable to protect his people? If Jesus truly was ruler of heaven and earth, why did Rome prevail? Why was his apostle in jail? Why did the clouds of darkness cover the face of the earth? The imprisonment of John was more than a human tragedy; it was a theological dilemma, the contradiction of all they believed, for the imprisonment of John seemed to prove that Jesus was *not* Lord. Jesus was *not* able to protect his people! And the people were pushed into discouragement, on the brink of despair, ready to abandon the faith and turn to the worship of Caesar instead.

To that problem John must write out of his prison cell on Patmos. To a people who felt they were abandoned by God, to a people who were tempted to believe that they lived in a world ruled by the devil himself and not by God, he had to pen a message of comfort and assurance. He had to review and interpret their suffering for them. He had to clarify the issues, making it abundantly clear that things were not what they seemed. That God had not abandoned them, that despite the evidences all around them, the earth was indeed the Lord's and the fulness thereof. That the final word, the ultimate power, was of God and not of Rome.

The people were taking their plight of persecution as evidence of God's inferiority, of his inability to protect and deliver his own, as proof of the supremacy of the God-opposing forces. And John must write not only a letter of encouragement and comfort, but he must do more than that—he must interpret their suffering to them in such a way that they could see that their agonies were not the evidence of God's impotence but a sign of his power. Things were not what they seemed! Their trials and troubles did not prove that God was helpless to intercede and deliver them, but rather those trials and troubles were of God himself, designed to purify and perfect them. He had to make it clear that the persecution was not, as it seemed, an evidence of God's abandonment, but instead a proof of his power, a sign of his lordship.

How John does that we will see when we move into the main body of his letter itself. But for the moment we look only at how his setting, his situation, is going to determine the form of his letter, is going to shape for him the way in which he expresses himself. Remember, he is a prisoner. Remember, he is sitting in a Roman jail and any letter he writes is going to be read by the censors. He is going to be forced by his circumstances to use the message and manner of apocalyptic writing which the Jews had developed earlier. Of course, he will not have to, or won't be able to, use pseudonymity. There will be no necessity or possibility of passing off his writing under an assumed or fictitious name, for his Roman jailers will know who wrote the letters he asks them to deliver. That part of apocalyptic practice he can abandon. He can say, flatly and unambiguously, in his opening lines, who he is and where he is: "I John, your brother, who share with you in Jesus the tribulation . . . was on the island of Patmos. . . ." (Rev. 1:9). That much of apocalypse can fall by the wayside. There is no need, indeed, no possibility, of concealing who he is. His prison cell makes that impossible.

But the rest of apocalyptic he can and does employ. He writes in deliberately disguised language. He resorts to imagery the Romans will not understand. He cannot write in a literal and obvious way. He cannot say in clear and unambiguous terms what lies closest to his heart. What would happen if he wrote what he believed, that Domitian was a blasphemous son of the devil himself? What would happen if he cried out that the Roman empire, in its demand that men bend down and worship Caesar, was a diabolical scheme of Satan himself designed to win men away from Jesus? The letter would never be delivered. It would never clear the censors.

And thus he must camouflage and conceal his true meaning. He must resort to non-literal symbolism, to obscure and apparently meaningless references which his Roman censors would see merely as the senile musings of a mad old man. He must talk of drunken harlots and beasts which rise up out of the sea and angels and demons who traverse heaven and sea dumping bowls of wrath on the heads of men. To the practical tough-minded Roman jailers those bizarre images could easily be dismissed as the rantings of a man gone berserk, as the senseless ravings of a lunatic, and the letter could thus get by the censors.

But the people back on the mainland, hopefully *they* would have the eyes to see what the Roman jailers could not see! Hopefully *they,* with their Christian background and their awareness of the earlier apocalyptic message and manner of expression, would recognize that things were not what they seemed, that what he was talking about behind those grotesque images and that bizarre symbolism was in reality a message of comfort and assurance, an affirmation that the power of Rome would not prevail. *They* were supposed to see that he was not really talking in a literal way about a drunken harlot or a celestial battle unrelated to the human scene —he was talking about Rome. Rome would fail. God would prevail. Christ *was* in charge, despite the testimony of the circumstances.

John's imprisonment on the island and their persecution on the mainland were not to be seen as an evidence of God's impotence. Not at all. God was in charge, not Caesar. But that could not be said clearly and flatly, or the letter would never be delivered. He had to write in symbolism, in cryptic and disguised terms, in apparently meaningless vagaries and ramblings easily dismissed as nonsensical ramblings by the practical tough-minded Roman jailers.

Thus any attempt to read the book of Revelation in a

literalistic or wooden way is forever doomed to failure. Any attempt to take the book literally fails to recognize the circumstances under which it was written, and why the author was forced to purposely cloak his message of comfort in disguised language.

Let us look at some specific examples of what we are talking about. In Rev. 14:1 and 14:3 John speaks about the elect of God as being one hundred and forty-four thousand in number, "the hundred and forty-four thousand who had been redeemed from the earth." Some sectarian groups take that number literally, and assume that in the final company of heaven there will be precisely that number saved. They take the number literally, and they limit those saved to that figure. To take the number literally is to come to the exact opposite conclusion that John the author is trying to get across.

How many tribes in ancient Israel? Twelve. And how many disciples did Jesus choose as basis of the new Israel, the church? Twelve. And what is 12 x 12? 144! Now, before we go any further we must remind ourselves of how the ancient Jews thought, of a characteristic of their mental patterns, for John was a Jew. How did the Jew express infinity, a large and endless number? By simply multiplying the number by ten! When Peter asks Jesus, "How many times should I forgive my brother, seven times?", Jesus answers him "I do not say to you seven times, but seventy times seven" (Matt. 18:21-22). What does Jesus mean? Is he to be taken literally? Is Peter to walk about with a pad of papyrus and a pen in his hand, marking down the number of times he forgives his fellow man, and when he arrives at 490 times he can stop forgiving? Of course not! Jesus is not to be taken literally here. He is speaking concretely, as a good Jew would. He is simply trying to get across the idea of infinity, of an endless series, of a continuing never-ending act of forgiveness, by multiplying by ten.

And that is what Rev. 14:1 and 14:3 are attempting to say. How many will be saved? A specific limited number confined to a mere and literally understood 144,000? Not at all! What John is saying, to a discouraged and persecuted people, on the brink of despair, tempted to believe that all is lost and God will not be able to deliver his people, is that not a one shall be lost. That God's power is sufficient to deliver *all* who call on his name. That all the sons of the old covenant, the remnant of the twelve tribes of Israel, and all the followers of the new Israel, adherents to the teachings of the twelve apostles, that all of them, 12 x 12 = 144 x 10 x 10 x 10, that all of them shall be rescued by the redemptive power of God! To take the number literally, to *limit* it, is to come to exactly the opposite conclusion intended by John. He is seeking to tell of the *unlimited* power of God.

Another example. In the closing chapters of the book is the repeated affirmation that Christ will reign a thousand years, and reigning with him will be his elect. In Rev. 20:2-3 we read that Satan shall be shut away for a thousand years and during that time Christ shall rule. And then at the end of the thousand years Satan "shall be loosed for a little while." And Rev. 20:5-7 again refer to the thousand years of Christ's reign. There are those who take that number literally, who approach the book in a literalistic and futuristic way, who see the book as a forward glance down to the end of time as a glimpse of what things are to be like in the future, and anticipate that at the end of the age there shall be a millenium, a thousand years, when Christ's rule shall cover all the earth.

Those sectarian groups, who take this line of interpretation, really cannot be sure from the way the book expresses itself, just exactly when the beleagured church will be lifted up to glory. Will it be before or after the thousand years? And thus we have pre-millenial interpretations, and post-millenial interpretations! *All* of those interpretations are perversions and misconceptions of what John is saying! The number is not to be taken literally, pointing to the future, indicating a specific and limited time in which the glory of God will be seen as sovereign for a concrete period of time. On the contrary, John is insisting that God is in charge, Jesus is always in charge, He is indeed ruler! The confession of the earliest church, "Jesus is Lord!" is true despite the apparent evidence to the contrary!

The persecution of the church, the persecuting havoc caused by Domitian, is not a sign of Satan's superiority. Christ *was* and *is* and *will be* in charge—he is the Alpha and Omega, the beginning and end, *all* things unroll under him! His rule is eternal, endless, not confined to a limited period at the end of the age, but infinite, 10 x 10 x 10! To take the number literally, as referring to a specific moment at the end of the history of this world is to pervert the intention of the author. He is not saying that Christ *will be*, later, in command. He is saying that *right now,* now and forever, Christ is in charge.

And that is the way that the "loosing of Satan for a little while" is to be understood. That is not some specific period in the distant future when his diabolical power will be felt. That period is *now!* Right then and there, in the wrath of Domitian, the fury of Satan is being seen. But, do not despair. Do not give up the faith. Do not assume that Satan is in control, that Rome is ruler of all. Satan acts only with God's permission. He is being loosed, he is accomplishing God's purposes. It is *God,* not Satan, who rules the world and stands behind the suffering of the elect on the mainland.

4

Letters to the Seven Churches

The first three chapters of Revelation are introductory. Introductions can be of two types. Those which are casual, serving merely as the opening of the door, bearing no vital relationship to the real heart of the matter to come later in the main body of the work. And those which are absolutely essential, laying out in embryonic fashion the very essence of all that is to follow. Revelation's three chapters of introduction are of the latter type. Every great theme of the book is already found in compact and concise form, in these opening letters to the seven churches. If one understands the introduction, one has greatly grasped the essential ideas of the entire book.

Everyone who has ever read carefully the Gospel of John is aware of the peculiar style of that writing. It is circular in style. It can be compared to a spiral staircase. The reader revolves again and again around repeated themes. The author of the Gospel of John takes up an idea, examines it intensely, and then lays it down and moves to another theme, only to later return, like a spiral staircase, to the theme he examined earlier, this time examining it more intensely, only from a slightly different point of view. There really are not very many different themes in the Gospel of John. Instead, only a few themes, each examined, laid aside, returned to later from a heightened and altered point of view and examined anew from this revolving heightened perspective, much like mounting that winding, climbing, staircase, looking at the same thing, but always from a changing viewpoint.

The book of Revelation has the same structure. We turn now to examine some of the details of the first three chapters, commonly called "the letters to the seven churches," before we turn to overall evaluation.

First, as we noted, the author identifies both himself and his place of writing in 1:9. He is John, and he is imprisoned on the rocky fortress island of Patmos, just off the Asian coast, not far from Ephesus where he had earlier ministered.

And the audience is also identified. In 1:4 he tells us to whom he writes, "the seven churches that are in Asia," the people back home, the mainland church passing through the same persecution which has pushed him into prison on Patmos. The seven churches are located in (1) Ephesus, 2:1, (2) Smyrna, 2:8; (3) Pergamum, 2:12, (4) Thyatira, 2:18; (5) Sardis, 3:1, (6) Philadelphia, 3:7, and (7) Laodicea, 3:14. Notice well, these are not all the churches in that part of the world. For example, we know that not far from Ephesus, several miles up the Lycurgus river valley there was another flourishing church at Colossae. And there were other churches in the area too. In other words, the identifying of the churches by picking out but seven tells us something of the author's use of numbers.

He pours an enormous symbolical significance into his numbers. Seven, in this book, is always the sign of completeness. Seven for the Jew was the sign of fullness, of totality. The number is not to be taken literally, as if his audience was limited. The number is expressive of all the churches in the area. To take the number literally instead of illustratively is to limit the author's intention and the audience's scope, whereas it is his intention to address the entire church! Seven is enough, seven is sufficient, because seven represents fullness, completeness, totality.

Perhaps the significance of seven becomes clearer when we see to what it is contrasted. Anything which falls short of seven, which comes up only six, is incomplete, false, trying to intrude on the fullness of God, an impostor falling short of fullness. That is the significance of the allusion later on in Rev. 13:18. There the image used for the persecuting Rome, seeking to force the church to worship it and cast a pinch of incense on the altar of Domitian, is a beast, a beast with a number, and the number is 666, not one 6 but three 6's. Rome claims to be divine, Rome demands worship. But Rome falls short of the mark. It is a false claimant to deity. It does not have the fulness of glory of God himself. To yield to Rome is to bow down to the impostor.

Additional details. Notice the constant affirmation, found in almost every one of the seven letters, of the *present* fact of God's omnipotence and all-affecting power. The rule or reign of God is not a future hope, an anticipated or coming sovereignty, but it is instead a *present* fact. It is not in some future millenium, some coming span of a thousand years, when God will reign. But it is *now* that God rules. The afflictions and persecutions poured out on the church are not a sign of God's impoverishment or the people's abandonment, as the people on the mainland were tempted to view them, but those sufferings must instead be seen as the work of God. It is God who rules, right now, in the midst of the trials. Notice, for example, 1:5, the insistence that Jesus is "the ruler of kings on earth." Rome is not an independent enemy, acting in opposition to God. The trials of the time are not an indication of the supremacy of the opposition and the frailty of God. It is Jesus himself who rules all things. Somehow, the people on the mainland must be forced to view their sufferings from this other point of view, not seeing their troubles as a sign of God's impotence but as an evidence of God's will.

Rev. 1:15 also insists that Jesus "*has* freed" them. Even now, at that moment, they stand exposed only to God in action. He is the one to whom they must account, to God alone. Rev. 1:8 insists on the same truth. Jesus and Jesus alone is in charge, he is the ruler of all things, he is the "Alpha and Omega [the first and the last letters of the Greek alphabet, the one who encompasses all communication, the Word of God, the only voice to be heard!] . . . who was and is and who is to come!" The obvious emphasis is on the enduring, eternal, never ending and immediate nature of Christ's rule. The churches dominated by Domitian must see that Domitian has no power of his own. Christ alone commands the cosmos.

Coupled with the repeated affirmations on the supremacy of God are the constant assurances that those who hold firm and do not fall faint, who do not compromise and go to the other side, will triumph. In 2:7 we read,

"To him who conquers I will grant to eat of the tree of life." That is, the trials are not negative but positive. God has a purpose in them. Those who endure have a prize laid up for them. Things are not what they seem. This is not the affliction of the enemy, but the opportunity of God. Those who belong to Christ shall be more than conquerors if they but stand firm in the faith: "He who conquers shall not be hurt by the second death" (Rev. 2:11). See also the same promise in 2:26, "He who conquers and who keeps my works until the end, I will give him power . . .", and 3:11, "I am coming soon; hold fast what you have, so that no one may seize your crown. He who conquers I will make him a pillar in the temple of my God; never shall he go out of it. . . ."

This is not an easy thing to see. The mainland church is sorely tried to see the sufferings as a curse, as an evidence of the enemy's malignant might, rather than seeing those sufferings as a sign of God's cleansing purpose. And thus these early letters are sporadically punctuated by an appeal to pierce beyond the surface of things and to use divine wisdom, to see these things as God sees them, to recognize them as blessings, not banes. Hence the appeal, again and again, "He who has an ear, let him hear!" (Rev. 2:11, 2:17, 2:29, 3:6, and other places). Things are not what they seem. It is God, not Rome or Satan, in charge of all things. Wake up, see that fact. If you have ears, listen to what I am telling you! The enemies of God do not rule the world. It is Christ who rules over the nations! If you stand firm in that faith you too shall be more than a conqueror.

And notice, especially, the one verse at the end of the seven letters which makes that thought abundantly clear,

Rev. 3:19: "Those whom I love, I reprove and chasten: so be zealous and repent."

That is the key. They are a sinful church in need of reproof and purgation, punishment for cleansing. And this meaning is found not merely in a few isolated details of fragmented phrases of these seven introductory letters. Instead, that theme dominates the fabric and framework of the entire three chapters. Notice well that there is a precise pattern to those seven letters. They see their suffering as a proof of the impotence of God. John sees their suffering as the will of God. God is in command. Why, then, are they suffering? Because God has willed it, willed it for chastening, for reproving, for cleansing. There is method in his seven letters, a definite pattern, an emerging emphasis.

The series of seven letters begins with much praise and a little rebuke. In the first letter, to Ephesus, 2:1-11, the praise or the affirmation dominates. "I know your works, your toil and your patient endurance, and how you cannot bear evil men." Much praise. But still not a perfect church, and thus comes the rebuke, "But I have this against you, that you have abandoned the love you had at first. Remember, then, from what you have fallen, repent, and do the works you did at first" (Rev. 2:4-5).

That is the pattern of the first of the letters, much praise with an occasional rebuke. The praise dominates. Indeed, in the second letter, to Smyrna, Rev. 2:8-11, the rebuke does not even appear. But it is usually present, though not central. In the third letter to Pergamum, the audience there too, despite their contribution, is reminded that "I have a few things against you . . ." (Rev. 2:14). Notice especially, in the rebuke to Thyatira in the fourth letter, the flat and unqualified insistence that their suffering is not the work of the devil but the will of God himself. After the phrase of 2:20, "But I have this against you'" indicating their sin, comes the insistence that it is God who punishes! "I gave her time to repent, but she refuses to repent. . . . Behold, I will throw her on a sickbed . . . I will strike her children . . . I will give to each of you as your work deserves" (2:21-23).

And then Sardis is told, emphatically, in the face of their feeling that their woe is evidence of God's failure to protect them, that such is not at all the case. It is they, not God, who are falling short. "I have not found your works perfect" (3:2), therefore ". . . repent. If you will not awake, I will come like a thief . . ." (3:3).

As one moves through the seven letters, the pattern becomes ever clearer. The church stands in need of a visitation of wrath, in need of a purging punishment of God which will wash away their evil! And that climax is clearly seen in the final of the seven letters. What begins with an emphasis on endurance, an affirmation of faith, tinged with an occasional rebuke, steadily sees a shift of emphasis until we get to the final letter in which all praise has disappeared and there stands alone a searing indictment of sinfulness. In that final letter, not one single word of fidelity, but judgmental condemnation alone. In stinging words of caustic rebuke, the veil of feigned piety is stripped away and Laodicea is laid bare! "I know your works; you are neither cold nor hot. Would that you were cold or hot! So, because you are lukewarm, and neither cold nor hot, I will spew you out of my mouth" (Rev. 3:15-16).

To a people suffering, and seeing their suffering as

undeserved, an evidence of God's impotence, John thunders that things are not what they seem. The self-pitying church, priding itself on its fullness and chiding God for his failure to protect, is slashingly told they are not perfect. They have forgotten their first love. They need to repent, or they will be hit even harder, they will be spit out of the mouth of God, rejected!

This is a harsh word, an unexpected rebuke, a stinging reversal of what they believed! They had thought that their trials were undeserved, a contradiction of their convictions, an evidence of God's inability to rescue them. They were a self-pitying people, bordering on the brink of despair, entirely convinced that the failure was on God's part. He had let them down. He had not come through for them and lifted them out of the hand of the enemy. And that self-righteous church is told in no uncertain terms that the problem rests in them and not in God!

Yes, they are right. God stands at the end of the process. Yes, one day they shall be lifted up out of suffering and sing the songs of the saved at the end of the age. But no, they are wrong, God does not stand only at the end of the process. He rules a thousand years, forever and forever, now as well as then, and the crucible in which they are being pounded is not an evidence of God's impotence but a measure of their own evil. The judgment has been spoken. They must be punished until they repent. The judgment having been spoken, the punishment can now begin. And the chapters which follow describe that punishment—describe it as the will of God, not the work of the enemy.

5

The Four Horsemen—Avengers Sent by God

In chapters 1 through 3 we saw that John the Apostle was insisting that the church needed cleansing. It was not a perfect church. God had certain things against it. It had lost its first love. It had become lukewarm, worthy only to be spit out of the mouth of God. Out of this grew John's basic insistence that God would punish the church to purge it, afflict it in order to cleanse it. That is the thought, the whole thought—nothing more than that, but nothing less than that—expanded in the next eight chapters, chapters 4 through 11, to which we now turn.

Events on earth, reviewed in the first three chapters, demand that God enter in judgment. And thus, after the first three chapters of reviewing the unfaithfulness of the church on earth, the scene shifts heavenward. The apostle's eyes are lifted up and he begins, in chapter 4, a description of the exalted majesty of God, a holy God who cannot have fellowship with that which is unholy. The entire fourth chapter is an impressive recounting of the sovereignty of God, adored and revered by all about him. The vision or description begins by elaborating the furniture of heaven, the throne of God high and lifted up, made of jasper and emerald (4:1-6).

Behind these concrete images of physical wealth, the spiritual thought which is intended to emerge is that the things of God are unlike the things of the world. God and man are cut from different cloth. God is rich, overflowing, but man is impoverished. The physical image is intended to evoke the obvious spiritual parallel. Faith in God, trust in his omnipotent sovereignty, allegiance to his will, those things abound on the heavenly scene. There he is adored. But not on earth! In heaven, the angels of God, the living creatures that surround the throne, are crying out night and day, never ceasing, their refrain "Holy, holy, holy is the Lord God almighty" (4:8). On the heavenly scene, those who follow in God's train say without ceasing all the day long, "Worthy art thou, our Lord and God . . ." (4:11). That is the way it is in heaven. But always, in the light of the first three chapters, we are reminded that it is not that way on earth. That is the way it ought to be on earth. His saints on earth should adore him below as the angels do above. But that is not the way it is. On earth, love has dimmed, allegiance has become lukewarm, God has several things against the church which must be dealt with in a dire way. God must act to cleanse, and the cleansing begins in chapter 5.

In the first verse of chapter 5 we see the scroll, the roll call of the people of God on earth. Here in the scroll are recorded the conduct of the people, the deeds of the saints. They thought their record. was impeccable, but the seven letters to the churches made it clear that this was a delusion of their pride. They are *not* perfect, heaven knows that, and now *all* will know that, for the book will be opened and their sorry record will be exposed to all, their need for punishment will be made a matter of public record.

Note well the ironic allusion to their illusion, to the church's self-deception. At first, it appears, no one can open the scroll, thus their great virtue will go unnoticed and unrewarded, and there is weeping on the earth (5:4). The sheer irony of it! The dramatic juxtaposition of the smug self-congratulating pride of the church, convinced of its own perfection, weeping that its good deeds might go unnoticed, counterpoised to the actual reality, they are a sinful church and when the book is opened their infidelity will be revealed. They are weeping for fear that the book will never be opened, and they ought be shuddering in fear in the light of the fact that the book will be opened.

The suspense builds. The book of Revelation is dramatically written, a superb work from the literary point of view. It begins with the setting of the people, persecuted under Domitian, ready to find fault with God and accuse him of having abandoned them, failing to protect them. Then in the first three chapters the apostle insists that things are not what they seem, the church is guilty of losing its zeal, and their persecutions are not a sign of God's abandonment but of his wrath and their need for cleansing. Then comes chapter 4, the dramatic pause which shifts the eyes heavenward, showing how things are above as opposed to things on earth. Above, God is adored and worshipped. Below, there is a lukewarm church. Then in chapter 5 the scroll appears and the church weeps because the assumed righteousness of the church might not be made manifest to all. But always the author is moving toward his own insistence, that when the scroll is opened the true nature of the church will be revealed, and then, after the scroll is opened—not before when its contents are still secret, will be the time for weeping. It will be the time for weeping, because then the entire cosmos will know what God already knows: his church has failed him, rather than the other way around, and God will have to punish them.

Who is right? The people who claim perfection and see their troubles as a sign of God's failure? Or John who insists that the people are far from perfect and their troubles come from a righteous God? The opening of the scroll is the critical issue. That will reveal who has the proper view of the trials of the church.

In chapter 6 the answer comes. John is right. One seal is opened, only one at first, and that by itself is sufficient to make the issue clear, sufficient to make clear from whom comes the affliction, from Rome the enemy of God acting in opposition to God, or from God who uses Rome merely as a means, an instrument. The answer comes. The first seal is opened, 6:1, and, 6:2, the first of the feared four horsemen of the Apocalypse is sent forth, raining terror on the earth. He is sent *of God.*

And again and again and again the sequence is repeated. In 6:3 another seal is opened on the heavenly scene, and in 6:4 another of the four horsemen is sent out by God, taking "peace from the earth, so that men should slay one another." And then in 6:5 the third seal is opened, and in 6:6 the third rider goes forth to afflict the earth, and there is famine and deprivation in abundance. And in 6:7 the fourth seal is opened, and in 6:8 the fourth horse gallops out "to kill with sword and famine and with pestilence."

Behind the multiple images, we cannot always be sure of the specific meaning of any one given incidental detail, but the overall thought is unmistakably clear, that the trials and troubles of the church on earth originate with God. It is he who commissions the riders to their task, it is from heaven that they come forth. Any other interpretation is untrue to the text as it stands. It is a tremendously uncomfortable conclusion for us to come to today, and even more shattering for the people who heard it for the first time, but uncomfortable or not, no honest reading of the text can escape the clear and unqualified insistence of the writer that the chaos and calamity to which the church is exposed comes from the throne of heaven itself.

In the middle of chapter 6 references to the horsemen cease, but the catastrophes continue. Earthquakes, 6:12. Cringing fear on the face of the earth, 6:15. And always it is the *wrath of the Lamb* which is being exercised (6:16).

In the midst of these frightful calamities originating with God, the author must pause to make clear once more his understanding of why God is doing this. Not to cripple or maim or destroy, but to purge, to cleanse, to re-establish a wayward church on the right way. Thus in chapter 7 he reminds the seven churches that they need not despair, that the true saints of God are sealed and will survive, that 144,000 will triumph. They will pass through the purging fires and be burned clean. They will eventually see the righteousness of God's ways and cry out, "Amen! Blessing and glory and wisdom and thanksgiving and honor and power and might be to our God for ever and ever! Amen." They will, having suffered, be like the heavenly creatures described in chapter 4, ready to praise the name of God without ceasing. They will "come out of the great tribulation" purified, with their robes washed white, made clean (7:14), and, having passed through the ordeal and having been cleansed, they will need to suffer no more for their suffering will have accomplished its purpose. For them, suffering will be ended and they can join the saints of heaven sitting around the throne of God (7:15), knowing no more the trials of the flesh. "They shall hunger no more, neither thirst any more; the sun shall not strike them, nor any scorching heat. For the Lamb in the midst of the throne will be their shepherd, and he will guide them to springs of living water; and God will wipe away every tear from their eyes" (7:16-17).

But always, we are reminded in the opening letters to the seven churches, this cleansing of the elect will come only through repentance, through the acceptance of the chastisement as the deserved punishment of a holy God: "Those whom I love, I reprove and chasten; so be zealous and repent" (3:19). Chapter 7, then, is the pause which reminds them of the purpose of the affliction, to bring about repentance, and the promise of what repentance will bring—a purged church freed of all further suffering, fellowshiping before the throne of the Father, one with the heavenly creatures above in undivided allegiance.

At the end of the pause in chapter 7 indicating anew the purpose of the punishment brought to a close, the author is able to turn once more to his thought of chapters 5 and 6, that the punishment is indeed from God, not from the enemies of God.

In chapter 8, seven angels stand before God (8:2). Remember, the number seven is symbolic, signifying completeness. From the seven shall come the complete purging punishment of God. In 8:4-5, one of the angels who stands before God comes forth, takes the censer, and throws it on earth, and there are peals of thunder, flashes of lightning, and earthquakes. Then one of the other angels before God, one of the seven, blows his trumpet (8:7), and immediately "there followed hail and fire, mixed with blood, which fell on the earth; and a third of the earth was burnt up, and a third of the trees were burnt up and all green grass was burnt up."

Then come the other seven angels of God, each blowing his trumpet, each acting on behalf of God, each causing havoc on the face of the earth. In 8:8 we read that the second angel causes the sea to turn putrid. In 8:10 fire falls from heaven. In 8:12 darkness covers the face of the earth. The activities of the angels produce catastrophic results: "the earth burnt up . . . sea became blood . . . many men died . . . light was darkened. . . . Woe, woe, woe to those who dwell on earth, at the blasts of the other trumpets which the three angels are about to blow" (8:7-13).

The same unrelenting tempo, the same concentration on catastrophe, periodically punctuated with the insistence that it is God who stands behind the calamities, dominates chapter 9 as well. In 9:13 "a voice from the four horns of the golden altar before God" issues the command that a third of mankind is to be put to death (9:15), and then we are again reminded, in 9:20-21, why the havoc continues—"nor did they repent. . . ."

Because they did not repent, because the promised restoration outlined in chapter 7 cannot yet take place, the punishing purgation, the heaping of woe upon woe, must yet continue. And continue it does in chapter 10. In 10:11, the seer on Patmos is told, "You must again prophesy about many peoples and nations and tongues and kings."

Why many peoples and nations and tongues and kings? Why must the affliction be universal, rather than confined to a wayward church? Because the enemies of the church are making the same mistake as the church. They too are interpreting the sufferings of the church as a sign of God's impotence. The church, battered under Domitian, was interpreting their trial as undeserved, an indication of God's inability to protect them. And precisely the same conviction dominated the enemies of the church, the nations and the kings. They too assumed that the God of the church was feeble. They too saw in their ability to afflict the church with various ills a sign of their own power. They too assumed that they were independent entities in opposition to the will of the God of the church. They, therefore, must suffer as well. They must be taught humility! They must recognize that they, like Pilate, had no power except that which was given from above. They are but servants, forced even against their will, to accomplish the purposes of God. Things are not what they seem. The enemies of the church rejoice in their afflicting the church, assuming that this proves both their superiority, and the corresponding inferiority of the God of the people they are persecuting. But things are not what they seem. God is using them. They, even without their knowledge of the fact, are accomplishing his will, not theirs. It is his will that will be done, through them and despite them. And then, since they are enemies, they too will be afflicted. Thus the woes which afflict the church will be shared in by the enemies of the church. Devastation will be universal.

6

The War in Heaven— Satan an Enemy?

Our interpretation of Revelation to this point can be summarized in two statements. On the one hand, the people on the mainland, suffering under the persecution of Domitian, are pushed to the brink of despair. They see their suffering as a sign of God's impotence, his inability to protect them. They are convinced that the tragedies of their times are a sign of Satan's power. There is no hand of God in the present hour, no ear above to hear their plea. If God's helping hand is to be felt, it is not in the immediate hour but in the future that he will act. In the immediate hour the actor is Satan, and the church, the righteous church, suffers unfairly.

On the other hand, the apostle John in the prison on Patmos insists that even now God is in control. He rules for 1,000 years, and 1,000 years does not refer to some future limited slice of time. It is rather a concrete Jewish way of saying eternity, infinity, unending time. Jesus is even now ruling, he is the Alpha and Omega, always in charge. Thus the suffering of the church is not of Satan but of God. It is not to the future that they are to look for the evidences of God's actions. In their immediate suffering they are to see God. It is he, not Satan, who afflicts them. And he afflicts them because they are not a perfect church. They have become lukewarm, lost their first love, are in need of chastisement and purgation. Their suffering is not a sign of God's absence—it is a sign of their sin.

That interpretation poses two problems. The first problem is this: it appears to fly full in the face of what we said about apocalyptic literature. In Chapter Two we saw that the very heartbeat of apocalyptic literature was the concentration on the fall of Satan, the revolt of the angels. Apocalyptic literature was pessimistic, convinced that God was separated from this world and Satan was active here, in opposition to God, causing suffering among the saints. But apocalyptic literature was also optimistic in the sense that it awaited the future victory of God. The God-opposing forces causing suffering right now would be destroyed in the future when God re-established his rule. This is the viewpoint of apocalyptic literature. This is the viewpoint of John's people back on the mainland. But this is not the viewpoint of John on Patmos. How, then, can we call the book of Revelation an apocalyptic book when it seems to contradict the very essence of apocalyptic thought?

The second problem is this: the interpretation we have given to Revelation seems not only to contradict apocalyptic thought, but it also seems to contradict, or be contradicted by, the twelfth chapter of Revelation. In chapter twelve we seem to find pure apocalyptic thought, an excellent example of precisely what the people back on the mainland believe, an elaboration of satanic power, an insistence that suffering comes not from God but from God's enemy, the devil, an affirmation that God rules not in the present but only in the future when Satan will be destroyed. In Rev. 12:7 we find the explicit language of apocalyptic thought, speaking of the revolt of the angels: "Now war arose in heaven. . . ." The war is then described, and the enemy identified with a variety of titles, "the great dragon . . . that ancient serpent . . . called the devil and Satan, the deceiver of the whole world" (Rev. 12:9). And then Rev. 12:12 explicitly states that Satan, having been expelled from heaven, has come to earth where he wreaks great havoc. Heaven can rejoice, for it has been freed from his malignant presence. The devil has been cast out. But the earth is in for suffering, for that is where Satan has gone! "Rejoice, then, O heaven and you that dwell therein! But woe to you, O earth and sea, for the devil has come down to you in great wrath, because he knows that his time is short!" (Rev. 12:12). Here is, apparently, pure apocalyptic. Satan causing suffering in the immediate hour, his wrath is great—but God about to conquer him in the future, for Satan's time is short. Does not this language of chapter 12, insisting on Satan as an enemy, active in the present, to be destroyed in the future, contradict the interpretation we have given to the book?

Let us take these two questions, but in reverse order, dealing with the second one first: does not chapter 12 contradict what we have said about the proper understanding of Revelation? Does not chapter 12 see Satan as a real enemy, actively opposed to the will of God, exercising his own will, causing suffering? And therefore how can it be argued that John, on Patmos, is claiming that suffering is of God, not of the devil?

The answer to that problem can be found by reminding ourselves that there is a literary kinship between the book of Revelation and the Gospel of John. Clues for understanding the one can be found by studying the other. And, in the Gospel of John, one constantly recurring theme is the real key to the answering of the above question. That theme is this: God is in charge of all things. There are no independent powers working in opposition to God. God is sovereign, supreme—all things are his will, and even those who suppose themselves enemies of God are but servants of his will. Even those who rage most strongly seeking to thwart his will are but instruments of his purpose, doing precisely what God intends for them to do. It is God alone who acts. No independence is allowed to the enemies of God. Indeed, God has no enemies, only servants. Even those who resist his purposes are deluded in thinking they are resisting his purposes, for, even without knowing it, they are only his servants.

One can see this clearly, for example, in the eleventh chapter of the gospel. Here, Jesus has just raised Lazarus, an act which in many ways is the climax of the gospel. It is the final, seventh, sign manifesting Jesus' power. But it is also the climax not only of Jesus' disclosure of his power, it is also the climax of the resistance of the Jews. No sooner is the miracle of the raising of Lazarus accomplished than the religious leaders gather together in alarm to decide what to do: "What are we to do? For this man performs many signs. If we let him go on thus, every one will believe in him, and the Romans will come and destroy both our holy place and our nation" (John 11:47-48). Their meaning is clear. The Jews were a subject people, ruled by the Romans. And, as with all subject or enslaved people, there throbbed through their thoughts a hope of freedom, a readiness to revolt when it appeared there was reason to expect success.

And suddenly there appeared this Jesus with the power of God pulsating from his fingertips. Able to still the storms, cast out the demons, heal the sick, feed the multitudes, and now even raise the dead. Surely if there was anyone who could lift off their chest the accursed boot of Caesar, it was this man Jesus. The crowds began to look to him as a Jewish George Washington, one who could give them political independence, restore them as an independent nation (we are already told, in John 6:15, that many wanted to make him a political king). This is what the Jewish leaders see, and that is why they tremble! They are afraid that if Jesus is allowed to continue with spectacular acts like the raising of Lazarus the populace will become so excited that they will revolt against Rome. And the result will be tragic. They will not succeed. Rome will crush the uprising, "the Romans will come and destroy both our holy place and our nation."

Thus the high priest, Caiaphas, counsels them, and advises that the way out of the threat is to kill Jesus. If Jesus were destroyed, the political passions of the people would cool down, the possibility of revolt would pass, and the people would be preserved. Thus he counsels that ". . . it is expedient for you that one man should die for the people, and that the whole nation should not perish" (John 11:50).

Several things must be noticed here. First of all, notice that Caiaphas is speaking, apparently, as an enemy of Jesus. He is plotting Jesus' death, seeking a way to destroy Jesus. But notice also that even as he counsels how to destroy Jesus he summarizes the very essence of Jesus' purpose—the innocent One will die that the nation might live! In one explosive phrase, he summarizes the entire purpose of Jesus' life. Now is that just coincidence? Is it to be dismissed as merely a remarkable accident that the enemy of Jesus ends up epitomizing the purpose of Jesus? The author of the Gospel will not allow you to so dismiss it. The author flatly goes on to affirm about Caiaphas: "He did not say this of his own accord, but being high priest that year he prophesied that Jesus should die for the nation, and not for the nation only, but to gather into one the children of God" (John 11:51-52).

Here is a fundamental building block of the entire Gospel, the conviction that not even the enemies of God are in the deepest sense enemies of God. Even despite themselves, even without knowing it, they serve God's will. Even as Caiaphas thought he was speaking in opposition to the person of Jesus, he was speaking "not of his own accord" but being forced, as high priest, to prophesy, to speak a word for God summarizing the very purpose of Jesus. There is, in John, no power other than God's. There are no enemies, only servants. The servants themselves don't always recognize they are servants, but that alters nothing—they are instruments of God who is working his will through them.

This fact is seen not only in Caiaphas, but dominates all the Gospels, is clearly insisted on in each instance where we see someone who is superficially seen as an enemy of Jesus. Take, for example, Judas. Judas has always been seen as an enemy of Jesus, the betrayer, acting in opposition to Jesus' purposes. Not so in the gospel of John. In John chapter 13, Judas does not move a muscle until Jesus deliberately and explicitly turns to him and commands him, "What you are going to do, do quickly" (John 13:27). Judas is but a servant, God alone acts.

And what is true of Judas is true of Pilate as well. The arrogant Roman official is first confused, then infuriated, and finally frightened by the strange stance of Jesus in the trial scene. Jesus refuses to make a defense in his trial, as if he were remotely above the entire transaction. Pilate tries to bully him, force him into a response or a defense by reminding Jesus that Pilate has power: "You will not speak to me? Do you not know that I have power to release you, and power to crucify you?" (John 19:10). And then Jesus turns to him and makes Pilate quake with the majestic dismissal of disdain—"You would have no power over me, unless it had been given you from above . . ." (John 19:11). Pilate is but a puppet, a servant, an instrument, of the will of God. It is God, not Pilate, not Judas, not Caiaphas, who rules the present scene.

And precisely in that vein chapter 12 of the book of Revelation must be seen. There is no contradiction between this chapter and the interpretation we have given to the other chapters. From beginning to end of this book, it is God who is in command, it is his will that is being done. We are not to be misled by the language which seems to indicate in Rev. 12:7-12 that Satan is an independent force exercising his own malignant will in opposition to the purposes of God. On the contrary, he is but a servant of God, even as were Caiaphas, Judas, or Pilate, each of them unknown to themselves and despite themselves accomplishing the will of God. Satan is not an independent force, but a tool, an instrument of God's plan, and that is why Rev. 20:3 speaks of him as being tethered, tied up, bound, only to be "loosed for a little while." This is not John talking about some far distant future event on the rim of the eschatological horizon, an event which will take place at the end of time. He is talking about the present scene, the immediate hour. The church feels that God is not present. Their suffering is a sign of his abandonment. They are suffering unfairly and Satan is the active element in their world. If God is to act it will only be in the future for there is no evidence now of his might. And to this John answers that Jesus reigns 1,000 years—he always reigns! Pilate is not in charge. Caiaphas is not master of the situation. Jesus is not helpless in the hands of Judas! Things are not at all what they seem.

Jesus is the Alpha and Omega, the beginning and the end, the one constant God in Christ Jesus is always in command, 1,000 years! Not a limited period, but always. And Satan has no independent existence; he is but a servant in God's program. He seems to rage, to work in opposition to God, but in actual fact it is God who is working through him. It is, in fact, God who has loosed him in the present hour. He is sent forth, like the four horsemen, to cause suffering and pain, but he is loosed by God, sent forth by the Father, for it is the Father who stands behind the sufferings of the people on the mainland, chastising them for their sin, purifying them, using Satan as an instrument of that purification.

We began this chapter with *two* questions or problems: (1) does our interpretation of Revelation contradict the basic principles of apocalyptic literature?, and (2) does chapter 12 contradict our interpretation of Revelation?

We have answered the second question negatively. We have insisted that Rev. 12 does not deny or contradict our interpretation of Revelation, but on the contrary Rev. 12 must be seen in the light of our interpretation of the rest of the book. In Rev. 12, Satan is not to be seen as an independent enemy acting in opposition to God, but rather God alone is in command, now and forever, using even his supposed enemies to accomplish his will.

But to the first question an affirmative answer must be given. Yes, our interpretation of Revelation is in direct conflict with basic apocalyptic thought. Apocalyptic thought does see Satan as an independent enemy, but Revelation does not. Apocalyptic thought does argue that suffering is demonic, of the devil himself, but Revelation does not. Apocalyptic thought does insist that God's action is not a present fact but a future hope, but Revelation argues otherwise. Revelation does contradict apocalyptic thought.

In the deepest sense, we now have to modify or enlarge upon some of the comments we made earlier in Chapter Two. There we said that the book of Revelation is apocalyptic, that it has the marks of apocalyptic writing. Now we must add that Revelation is not *pure* apocalyptic. It takes up the *language* of apocalyptic or the *style* of apocalyptic, but it *abandons the content* of apocalyptic. John uses the same style of writing as apocalyptic, speaking in disguised and cryptic language, in symbolic terms, but he reverses and contradicts the very essence of apocalyptic thought, for apocalyptic thought affirms the idea of a world estranged from God, exposed to the evil will of God's enemies, a world to be rescued in the future by an eschatological intervention of God. And John in Revelation rejects each one of those ideas. The world is God's, his will is done here and now, not in the future alone, but always.

Indeed, one can take this a step further and insist that Revelation contradicts not only apocalyptic thought, but it contradicts as well much of what we find in the synoptic Gospels and in the Pauline epistles, for the synoptics and Paul adopt the apocalyptic view of the world, whereas John does not. This profound issue we will have to wrestle with in our closing chapter.

7

Cleansing Completed–
Paradise Restored

Chapters 13-19 of Revelation have the same basic thought as chapters 4-11. The woes of the saints are the will of God. Then, the final three chapters make clear the purpose of the persecution. The church is purged and cleansed, able and allowed to have fellowship with God in full. Those basic thoughts stand behind the multiple images of these many chapters.

The fundamental problem of most interpretations of this book is the assumption that the author has a wide variety of truths he wishes to express, a vast array of insights and exhortations. Not so. Such interpretations fail to recognize the spiral staircase style of the author of the Fourth Gospel, and the fact that we have here the same author at work. Hence the same style. There are differences of course. The Gospel's grammar is polished and near perfect, while Revelation is a coarse Greek. But that is because of the pressure of circumstances. The Gospel was honed and reworked for a long time, but the letter from prison was an urgently needed writing produced in haste, unpolished. And the type of language is also different. The Gospel is clear and lucid, with little obscure imagery and no bizarre or unusual figures of speech or allusions, while Revelation is nothing but the latter. But that too is because the author writes Revelation from a prison cell and must deliberately disguise his thoughts in order to clear the censors. Making full allowance for these differences, the fact still remains that Revelation is much like the Gospel, a spiral staircase style, a style in which there are very few themes, an absolute minimum of central ideas. It is a style in which those limited themes are reviewed again and again, each time from an altered or heightened perspective. An idea is introduced, laid aside but never abandoned, returned to in depth (or from greater height) later on. The substance, as in the Gospel, is tightly locked together. Each part hangs together with the whole, there are few loose ends. A theme of one section must be remembered when one reads another section. For example, the meaning of the whole letter is lost if the reader ever loses sight of the fundamental assertions of the seven letters in the first three chapters. The church was there described as lukewarm, waning in zeal, and we were told, "Those whom I love, I reprove and chasten; so be zealous and repent" (Rev. 3:19). The author lays aside that specific sentence, but never departs from its essential meaning. Indeed, all the woes that follow are but an elaboration of those opening ideas. The book, then, has no myriad of ideas, no wealth of varied content.

Failure to recognize that fundamental fact is precisely why many contemporary commentators find an incredible variety of meanings behind the multiple images of the book. The beast of chapter 13 can be Adolph Hitler, and Gog and Magog of chapter 20 can be Red China and Russia. Such interpretations are sheer nonsense, the uninspired phantasies of the interpreter himself. Certainly God could, if he would, unlock the events of the far future for his faithful, but would he? There is nothing in all of biblical literature to indicate that he would—no parallel, no precedent. God meets people where they are, in their own immediate existential circumstances, in the middle of their concrete problems and their needs, speaking specifically to their actual times in which they live. What good would it do to one under the sword of Domitian, threatened with death for his devotion to Jesus, to learn that perhaps in the year 1984 all of human history is to come to a close and Russia will use Egypt as a springboard to attack Israel? Those kinds of interpretations, like the church at Laodicea, ought to be spit out of one's mouth, distasteful and unacceptable. Exotic, yes; esoteric, yes; appealing to man's insatiable lust for glimpses of tomorrow, yes; but true to the thrust of all other Scripture, no! There are few thoughts in Revelation, not many, and the few that are found there speak with power and directness to the situation of those who first read the words.

Those few themes and ideas, and how they speak to the immediate audience of Asia Minor of 2,000 years ago, have already been stated and restated. But they must be summarized again, for they appear not only in what we have seen but in the balance of the book that follows.

(1) The people are being persecuted by the emperor Domitian who insists that they worship him as God.

(2) The people see that persecution of Domitian as an evidence of God's abandonment, or, conversely, as a sign of the strength of Satan, God's enemy. They are on

the brink of despair, tempted to believe that God is impotent, their faith futile, the enemy's might overwhelming.

(3) They are smugly self-satisfied, flattering themselves into believing that they are perfect, a fault-free church worthy of great blessing, desirous that their virtue might be known to all, that the book of their deeds be open to the world. Indeed, it is precisely their assumption of their own perfection which leads them to both resentment and despair due to their persecution. How could God abandon them, virtuous as they are? Unfair to them! Unworthy of God!

(4) Unwilling to give up entirely their faith in God, but unable to see the sign of his presence in their immediate affairs, they look for some future intervention of God. He is not acting now but surely he will plunge anew into human history in the final hour, destroy their foes, and rescue his people.

(5) John, however, imprisoned on Patmos, has a different view of the church's character. While he is entirely willing to acknowledge its good points, and thus sprinkles both his opening chapters and his later comments with observations of its fidelity, his overall verdict is that the church is far from perfect. Contrasted to the loyal celestial servants above, surrounding the throne of God, the church below is lukewarm, lacking in love, cooling in conviction, compromising its actions.

(6) Thus John also has a different view of the church's suffering. He sees it not at all as an evidence of God's abandonment but as a sign of God's visitation. Those whom he loves he chastens in order to purify.

(7) Therefore the church is wrong in confining God to the future alone. He is the Alpha and Omega, eter-

nally present, ruling a thousand years, forever and forever. He will be present in the future, but he is present even now, in their persecution. The trials and afflictions which they endure are his work and will.

(8) Rome, then, the persecuting power afflicting them, is but an instrument of God. Rome mighty Rome, proud and preening Rome, is not independent, holding sway over all the earth. Rome mighty Rome has no more power than Pilate the Roman had, only that given him from above. Rome is but an instrument of God's purpose, being used to chasten the church which Jesus loves so that church might repent and return anew to its original love.

(9) The author, however, cannot speak that message in clear and concise terms. He cannot disparage the assumed sovereignty of mighty Rome. He cannot dismiss it as merely an instrument in the hands of the God of the Christians. He cannot do that, for that would be not only ludicrous, it would be insulting! The proud Roman would find it on the one hand downright comic, laughable, that a persecuted prisoner sitting in an island fortress would make, in the light of his circumstances, such grandiose claims for his God. And insulting. That Rome mighty Rome is but a servant doing God's will—like Caiaphas and Judas and Pilate—is degrading. Thus if his letter is to clear the censors and be mailed on to the mainland, the author must cryptically disguise his language, write in symbols, speak of one thing when in fact he means something else. He can speak of harlots and blasphemous beasts, but behind the multiple images there stands Rome.

(10) To accomplish his purpose of writing in disguised language, he seizes on the time-honored practice

of Jewish apocalypse, perfected two centuries earlier in the persecutions under Antiochus Epiphanes. But even as he adopts apocalyptic style he adapts it. First of all, he does not have to write his message pseudonymously as did the earlier apocalyptic writers, for there is no need —indeed, no possibility!—of keeping his identity secret.

(11) He alters apocalyptic in even yet a more fundamental way. He reverses, even as he adopts the form, the basic idea of apocalyptic literature. Apocalyptic literature was written with one overriding conviction throbbing through it: the persecutions of the people were not the will of God but the work of the God-opposing fallen Satan, working through human powers such as Antiochus. That is the view of the mainland church as well, that Rome is a servant of Satan, that God is not active on the present scene. John rejects and reverses that idea. For him, the persecution of the church traces back to God, not to the enemies of God. The enemies are but servants. God is working in the present, not confined to the future. To look for him to rescue them in the future is to miss the entire point of the present persecution.

(12) The purpose of the present persecution is God's desire to bring the church to repentance, to purge it of all pride, to strip away its self-confidence and make it rely on God alone. The purpose of the persecution is to fulfill the phrase of the Lord's prayer, that God's will might be done on earth as it is in heaven. In heaven, the servants of God bow down in undivided adoration, worshiping his holy name without ceasing. On earth, the church is far from that ideal, and they must be chastened and reformed.

(13) But when the ordeal is over those who have endured and repented, those who have had ears to hear

and the wisdom needed to pierce through to the true motive behind their ills, will indeed be made like unto the heavenly host above. They too will enter into the full fellowship of the Father, tasting in abundant measure his mercy and love.

Those are the overreaching ideas of the letter from Patmos. Having reviewed them, we can now pursue them in the balance of the book.

Chapter 13, much like chapter 12, can easily be misunderstood. A superficial reading of it, out of context, could convince one that an independent enemy of God is persecuting the church. The beast rising up out of the sea, demanding that men fall down in adoration before it, is obviously and unmistakably a reference to Rome. Rome is across the water, a beast rising up out of the sea. And the demand for adoration is exactly the demand that Domitian is making. That much of the picture is clear. But, as said, the chapter is open to misreading.

One could consider, on the basis of this chapter alone, Rome to be an enemy, in opposition to God, working its own will, much as Satan in chapter 12 could be misunderstood as an independent enemy working his own will. The purpose of the persecution (is it negative and destructive, or positive and cleansing?) and the source of the persecution (is it from God or from the enemies of God?) are not made clear in this 13th chapter. All that is done is that, on the one hand, the persecution itself is described, and, on the other hand, there is the exhortation to hold on, not to give up, to endure: "Here is a call for the endurance and the faith of the saints" (13:10).

The same general remarks can be made about the

first half of the 14th chapter. Once more the sufferings are described, the tormentor is seen causing woe, and the call for endurance is once more repeated (14:12). However nothing is said about the purpose or origin of the woes. Are they positive, meant for good, stemming from God? Or evil, meant for destruction, deriving from God's enemies?

But then, in the middle of chapter 14, the thought of the earlier part of the book, when the four horsemen sent out from God were described, returns. The source of suffering is unmistakably identified. It is God who stands behind the afflictions of the hour. In 14:13 it is the "voice from heaven" which speaks and introduces the chaos soon to follow. And in 14:15 and 14:17 it is the angels of God who come "out of the temple," who rampage the earth with their devastating sickles. They are sent by God and the anguish of the earth is flatly and clearly traced back to God, for 14:19 unambiguously insists that all the woes thus far seen are because of the "wrath of God."

Once that idea is affirmed, the author never really departs from it in the next two chapters. One can dip down almost at will into nearly every verse of chapters 15 and 16, and in almost every case the one basic thought is that God is causing the woes. In 15:1 the portent or vision is a "portent of heaven," for it is there that the drama begins. It is God who is acting, and, in that very same verse, the unambiguous insistence of 14:19 is repeated. The plagues and catastrophes about to be spilled out are called "the wrath of God." There is no need for despair. There is no possibility of believing they have been abandoned of God, for he is present and active. But neither is there room for self-satisfaction or smug assumption of perfection, for God is present to judge and punish. The angels are about to spill out seven bowls of God's wrath.

But, again, though they are about to be punished, there is no room for despair on that count either, for the persecutions are drawing to a close. The number of the bowls is seven, and seven signifies completeness. The ordeal will soon end. If they but endure they will be enriched and purified. The wrath of God will not afflict them indefinitely, for full purging is now about to take place and, with the spilling of the seven bowls, the will of God will be accomplished and the suffering ended: ". . . seven plagues, which are the last, for with them the wrath of God is ended" (15:1).

But, though the end is in sight, they will have to endure (which is why the earlier two exhortations to endure were just uttered). They will have to endure, for the punishment of God is about to be poured out, the bowls of his wrath emptied onto the earth. In 15:7 once more the suffering, the woe, the wrath to be felt, is called "the wrath of God who lives for ever and ever." In opposition to the view of the church which sees God's rule only in the future, and the ills of the hour as a sign of God's absence, John insists that the wrath is of God, and God is for ever and ever, ruling now in their trials as well as in their future. Thus they must endure, submit.

And then again in 16:1, when the actual spilling out of the woes on the world begins, we are again reminded who controls the affairs of the world—not Rome, not the devil, for these are but servants. "Then I heard a loud voice from the temple telling the seven angels, 'Go and pour out on the earth the seven bowls of the wrath of God' " (16:1). God has spoken. What he has spoken must happen. Thus one after the other the angels spill out the bowls of wrath. In 16:2, 16:3, 16:4, 16:8, 16:10, 16:12, and 16:17 each of the seven angels under orders from God acts and all of nature goes awry. Suffering multiplies on the face of the earth. Rivers and fountains become blood (16:4). Every living thing that was in the sea dies (16:3). Fierce heat envelops the world (16:8). And on they go: blasphemy, the apparent triumph of evil, flashes of lightning and earthquakes. The entire cosmos reels.

Midway through the spilling of the bowls we are told that the process cannot stop. Punishment must be complete. All seven (signifying completeness) bowls must be spilled out. There can be no cessation of sorrow until the cup of God's wrath is drunk in full. Why? Because partial punishment would mean only incomplete cleansing. Limited affliction would not produce repentance and perfection. Thus, between the spilling of the fourth and fifth bowls, we are told the process must go on: ". . . and they did not repent and give him the glory" (16:9).

Again we must pause to remind ourselves that John is not writing of far future events. He is not describing some cataclysmic chaos surrounding the end of the world. These woes and pains are not something he foresees as happening at some later time. Behind his imagery and disguised language he is describing what is actually going on in that moment, and interpreting it for the church. They are, even then at that hour, experiencing the spilling out of the wrath of God.

Even as they read the letter they are under the sword of Domitian, but they did not repent. They did not give God the glory. They remain smug and complacent, satisfied with their own power and progress and fidelity. If there is any fault to be found it is not with them but with God for allowing them to suffer. And thus, because they still have not learned, the process must go on. To find the pogroms in Poland or the Inquisition in Spain or the massing of armies on the Manchurian border in these woes and trials is absurd. John's whole argument hinges on his conviction that God even now, at that precise moment, is alive and at work.

If it is true, and we insist that it is, that chapters 15 and 16 make clear that the source of the suffering is the wrath of God, then chapters 17 and following begin to interpret the purpose of the suffering. It is for cleansing, not for crippling. God chastens those whom he loves. He has a positive purpose at work. This is what rests behind the vision of chapter 17 and the later chapters.

In chapter 17 we are confronted anew with the same kind of logic we earlier described as characterizing the Gospel of John. There things were not what they seemed. Caiaphas appears to be an enemy of God, and yet "being high priest that year he prophesied," summarizing the entire meaning of Jesus' death, that the innocent should die that the nation might live. He acts as an enemy, but in reality he is a servant. Judas is but a tool in the hands of God. He tries to do evil, and he ends up accomplishing God's plan. Pilate struts and swaggers, and then is incredibly told that he is in reality a servant of the Most High!

Things are not what they seem. Enemy merges into servant, foe becomes in the profoundest sense friend, for he is working for the accomplishment of God's purpose. What appears in one way to be diabolical, opposed to God's will, is instead beneficial, a messenger of God. That appears to be the thought of chapter 17. Admittedly, it is difficult imagery and one cannot build an entire theology on it, but it does appear that behind the imagery those who hear the voice of God can see in the afflicting enemy what is really the servant of God. It takes great wisdom to see this, hence the mystery of the event is affirmed (17:7). But the chapter begins with a description of a harlot, apparently an enemy.

As the chapter unrolls the harlot, the wicked woman, is clearly identified with Rome (that is the meaning of the allusion to the seven hills—the site on which Rome was founded, 17:9). But, writing from a Roman prison, he cannot call her empire Rome, and must call it Babylon instead (17:5, 18:2, 18:21). And Rome's role as the cause of suffering is affirmed. Rome's war on the church underlies every sentence of chapters 17 and 18, but Rome's servanthood is affirmed as well. Rome does not exist independently. She is but an instrument. And when God's purging is complete the instrument will no longer be needed, and the harlot will be discarded, and all who put their confidence in her will be chagrined and dismayed (18:9). That is, the backsliding Christians of Asia Minor who did not endure, who yielded in the face of persecution, who buckled before the pressures of Domitian and sided with Rome against the gospel, will find they have chosen the wrong side. They are the ones who will find they have been deceived (18:23)!

Again, we are reminded that the immediate message is addressed to the immediate audience. John is not an idle speculator, whittling away at time heavy on his hands by exotically describing far future events. He is not preparing ammunition for some wild-eyed speculations of 2,000 years off so that men yet unborn can spy out modern politics cryptically revealed in sensational visions. He is instead somberly warning his seven churches that if they take things as they stand, they are mistaken. Things are not what they seem! Rome is not the power of the world. God is! And all those who apostasize, who give up the faith, who reject the church and place their confidence in Rome and put the pinch of incense on the blasphemous, adulterous altar of Domitian will discover to their horror—too late—that they have been deceived!

The enemy, Rome, is really a servant. And the punishments of the church are really a blessing, an opportunity for growth. That truth is not easily grasped, and certainly it was not grasped immediately by the church which is why all seven bowls must be spilled out, and why John must write his Revelation! But if they persist, if they endure, and if they repent and stand firm and do not go over to the other side, they will be cleansed. The imagery is fluid, and sometimes obscure in its individual detail, but the overall thought is quite clear. *God* is behind it all! He has commissioned the harlot, the beast. He holds Rome in his hand, "for God has put it into their hearts to carry out his purpose" and through the activities of these servants in disguise, these servants who work for God even without knowing it, "the words of God shall be fulfilled" (17:17).

All the blasphemers, all those who have capitulated in the face of Domitian's demands, all those who put their confidence in Rome and gave up the faith and abandoned the gospel, all will cry "Alas . . . alas!" in the end (18:10, 18:16, 18:19). They put their confidence in the great city, Rome, and their end shall be destruction, for they did not endure, they did not repent.

But on the other hand, those who do endure, those

who do not bow down in blasphemy to Domitian, who trust in God and not in the great city Rome, will be cleansed and redeemed. That is the thought which begins in chapter 19 and moves on into a crescendo in the final chapters of the book.

Even as the woes draw to a close, the church can begin to imitate the cry of triumph of the celestial servants on high. We recall that in chapter 4, when the woes were first about to begin, we saw the seer describing the loyal heavenly host, praising God without end. But, in chapter 4, that heavenly host was described in order to contrast it to the church on earth. In heaven, undivided obedience, continuing loyalty, unending praise and adoration of God. On earth, a lukewarm church cooling in its zeal. The description of the heavenly host in chapter 4 was for contrast, to show the difference between the servants above and the saints below. In chapter 19, we once more have a description of the loyal heavenly host above. But now things are different. Between chapters 4 and 19 the bowls of God's wrath have been spilled out. His cleansing has taken place. Those who have eyes to see and ears to hear, who heed the call to endure and do not submit to Domitian, who bend down to God in total obedience, will be cleansed. "God has put it into their hearts to carry out his purpose . . . the words of God shall be fulfilled."

Thus the heavenly host can be described again in chapter 19, but now no longer as a rebuke, now no longer to shame the church by the contrast between what they are and what they ought to be. Instead, now the heavenly host can be described anew to show them below what they are becoming, what God's intentions with them are. Now the description is made no longer to rebuke, but to inspire; no longer to emphasize the difference, but to emphasize the likeness. The mighty voice of the heavenly host is heard singing the praises of God, 19:1. Their enthusiastic affirmation of the goodness and power and supremacy of God reverberates throughout the heavens and evokes a corresponding echo from the saints below. They too, cleansed and purified, are now worthy of entering into that exalted fellowship.

The persecution is ended. God's purpose is achieved. The servants of his wrath can now be set aside, no longer needed. Satan can be cast into the lake of fire, dismissed, no longer necessary (20:10). He had been loosed, temporarily employed, along with the angels bearing the seven bowls of wrath, along with the four horsemen sent out from the temple, all of them servants, all of them causing pain. But now the purpose of the pain has ended, and the agents of affliction are no longer needed, for behold, all things have now been made new. Now the final verdict can be read! Now the book of the deeds of the saints can be rightly read (20:12).

In contrast to the smug complacency of the earlier church, proud but untested, eagerly clamoring for the opening of the book which would reveal their assumed virtue, now the book of the deeds of the saints can be rightly seen, and the names of those who endured will be read in the roll call of heaven. They are the ones who held firm, even unto death, and are redeemed. They are the ones, like unto the heavenly host above, who put God alone at the center of their existence, rejected the temptations of Rome, endured the cleansing afflictions of God, and now will be rewarded for their deeds: "And the dead were judged by what was written in the books, by what they had done" (20:11). Those who apostasized, who capitulated to Rome, will be like Rome, like Satan, set aside for they have no place in the kingdom of God (20:14-15).

But the emphasis in these closing chapters is not on the fate of the apostates, but rather on the reward of the faithful. The martyred church, the ones who continued their witness despite the temptations of the ordeal, are the ones who will taste the magnificence of God. For them, God needs no longer to act in wrath. He can reveal himself in his love. He has always loved them, but they did not always see that clearly, for they mistook his wrath as a sign of his impotence. They failed to see that the Lord chastens those whom he loves. But they have been chastened. They have endured, some even unto death. And now the reward is theirs: "and God himself will be with them, he will wipe away every tear from their eyes, and death shall be no more, neither shall there be mourning nor crying nor pain any more, for the former things have passed away" (20:3-4).

Then, in that glorious hour, their former afflictors can come forward and their servanthood of God be fully revealed by the fact that they are still carrying the instruments of anguish they caused, the bowls of wrath (21:9) and show the redeemed and cleansed saints the reward they have won. "Come, I will show you the Bride, the wife of the Lamb" (21:9). Their love earlier was cool, but it has been restored. The church is the bride, wedded anew to Christ, purged of sin and perfected in the purity of his purpose. Thus the glories of heaven, described in chapter 4 by images of material wealth, gold, precious gems, are once more described in chapter 21, again by images of material wealth, precious gems and priceless metals. But whereas the description was made in chapter 4 to shame the church (contrasting its poverty to the wealth of the saints above), now the description is made to show the rightful inheritance, the divine reward of the enduring church.

In contrast to their earlier state, when hunger prevailed, now the tree of heaven can bear "its twelve kinds of fruit, yielding its fruit each month" (22:2). It is the image of the Garden of Eden restored. Man in fellowship with God finds the goodness of God prodigal in its fullness, abundant to the extreme. Now John can return to the symbolism of the Gospel he had written earlier. In the second chapter of his Gospel, he told how Jesus had gone to a wedding feast attended by only a few persons. The crowd was so small that when Jesus arrived with his disciples it must have doubled the audience and exhausted the provisions, for they ran out of wine. Yet for that small company, for that mere handful of people, Jesus had turned 180 gallons of water into 180 gallons of wine (John 2:6). Wine in abundance!

The prophet Amos of old had yearned for the day when God would visit his people and make all things new, and in that glorious day of redemption, the superabundant fertility of the soil would be restored, the Garden of Eden would be renewed, the mountains themselves would flow with sweet wine (Amos 9:13). And at Cana the hopes and fears of all the years had been accomplished: 180 gallons, the mountains dripped with sweet wine, the Old Testament fulfilled, Eden restored. In John chapter 6 the multitudes had eaten their fill, and when all had been fed there remained 12 baskets of bread (John 6:13). All of Israel, all 12 tribes, had been fed, and there was much left over—such was the prodigal goodness of God. Eden was restored. In the presence of God there is plenty, more than enough.

And now that the persecutions have ended and accomplished their purpose, the tree of life can bloom anew bearing its fruits in all seasons. Hunger and pain and mourning and death are no more. "God himself will be with them. . . . And night shall be no more; they need no light of lamp or sun, for the Lord God will be their light, and they shall reign for ever and ever" (21:3, 22:5).

8

God and Satan—Some Biblical Views Compared

In this closing chapter we want to discuss two issues. The first is this: how are we to understand the fact that Revelation maintains a point of view opposite to that of apocalyptic literature and also opposite to the view of the synoptic Gospels and of Paul's letters? Does this not put Scripture into opposition with Scripture?

And secondly, what kind of comfort or hope is to be found in the portrait of God painted in Revelation, a God who chastises and causes woe? Is not this contrary to our conviction that God is love, compassionate, and concerned?

In discussing the first issue, the apparent contradiction between the parts of Scripture, the place to begin is with a simple yet far-reaching fact of language. Western civilization, our culture, is based on twin cornerstones—ancient Greek thought, and ancient Hebrew thought. But these two thought patterns were different. The Hebrew language was based on the verb. The Greek language was built on the noun. From that apparently trivial difference profound implications arise.

The Hebrew, for example, thinking in terms of verbs, asked the question, "What has God *done?*" He was concerned with action, deed, performance. The first sentence of the Bible begins with God in action, "In the beginning, God *created*. . . ." The Greek, however, thinking in terms of nouns, concentrated not on action, but on essence. Not on deed, but on nature, substance. The Greek would ask, "What is God *like?*" A sentence such as Gen. 1:1, "In the beginning God *created* . . . ," would be impossible for a Greek writer. He would have to begin by discussing the nature or substance of God, and only then would he be able to draw conclusions as to what God would do. Heraclites and Thales, for example, ancient Greek philosophers, debated about the *substance* of reality, fire or water. The Greek thought not in terms of verbs but in terms of nouns.

This fundamental difference could be developed in a variety of ways. It explains, for example, why ancient Hebrew language always had to be put into practice, had to be acted out, whereas ancient Greek thought was often content to simply believe something without necessarily practicing one's belief. This fundamental difference could also be used to help shed light on the supposed quarrel between science and religion, for it is Greek thought, based on the noun, which leads to science, and it is Hebrew thought, based on the verb, which leads to true religion. In pursuing the two avenues we would very soon be able to see that in the deepest sense there is no conflict between science and religion for they are but two complementary, not contradictory, ways of looking at life.

But space will not permit us to pursue either of those issues. The thing to concentrate on here is that Greek thought, built on nouns, leads to *logical* thought. But Hebrew thought, based on verbs, leads to *paradoxical* thought. The Greek thinks in terms of nouns. And nouns always act the same way. There is a constancy in nouns. Given elements have given properties that do not change. Water, for example, is always wet, and always flows. The noun, water, does not change. It might be hot or cold, but it has nonetheless given properties which never alter. This is the basis for logical thought. I go into a laboratory today and combine chemical A with chemical B at a given temperature in given amounts, and I get specific result. If I return to the laboratory tomorrow and combine the same two chemicals in the same amounts at the same temperature, I get the same result. That is *logical* or *consistent* thought. It is Greek thought, based on the noun. Things always act the same way, things are consistent. Since things are always consistent and logical, it follows that if I have a proposition or idea on one side that is true, which is contradicted by an idea on the other side, logically the second idea must be false. That is Greek thought, logical or consistent thought.

But the Hebrew does not think logically or consistently. He thinks paradoxically, because he thinks in terms of verbs. In paradoxical thought, opposites can stand together in tension. It does not follow that because proposition A is true, and proposition B is the opposite, therefore proposition B must be false. Not so, not when one thinks in terms of verbs. For example, say that a series of wonderful things happens to me on Monday. I get a promotion at work and a fine raise in pay. In addition, I win a new automobile because my credit card number was chosen by the Shell Oil Company. And on top of it all, my son wins a four-year college scholarship, so his major bills for the next four years are taken care of! Marvelous day! What kind of person will I be that day? I will be an absolute delight to be with! Anyone who runs across me that day will see by the way I act—by my verbs, by my actions—that I am a fine person, a joy to be with.

But then, to carry the illustration further, say that on Friday of the same week I lose my job, the car is repossessed, and my son flunks out of college. Now what kind of person will I be? Anyone who is with me that day will be convinced that I am an ogre, an unpleasant person to be with, an absolute boor! My verbs prove it. The way I behave reveals how distasteful I am!

Now, which one is true? Both are true! One day I am one way, another day another way! Both are true. My actions prove it. *That* is paradoxical thought, opposites held together in tension. And Hebrew thought is paradoxical.

The major problem in Bible study today is that all of us who have grown up in western, scientifically-orientated technological thought, are Greeks. We think in logical or consistent terms. Whether we have ever paused to ponder the fact or not is entirely beside the point. We are Greeks in our thinking. We assume that because proposition A is true and proposition B is the opposite, therefore B must be rejected as false. But the Bible was not written by Greeks. It was written by Hebrews, and if we would rightly read it, we must learn to think like Hebrews, learn to hold opposites together in tension. Because two ideas are in direct opposition, it does not follow that one is false and the other is true. Both can be true.

Countless examples of this fact can be given. What was Jesus, human or divine? The Greek church of the fourth and fifth centuries almost collapsed trying to answer that question. The Greek church almost collapsed because they were choosing one side or the other, Jesus was human *or* divine! The great Christological controversies which produced the creeds show the difficulty, indeed the near impossibility, of explaining in Greek terms how Jesus could be both human and divine. The Greeks thought in terms of nouns, substances, and it seemed logical and consistent to assume that if Jesus' substance was purely human, then it obviously could not be divine, or vice versa. Thus the Greek church went back and forth from one extreme to the other, arguing that Jesus was human or divine, but unable to explain how he could be both. The Hebrew never had a problem like that, because he thought in terms of verbs, not nouns. The Hebrew saw Jesus still the storm, walk on the water, heal the sick, raise the dead, and feed the hungry, and these mighty acts proved he was divine. But Jesus also wept when a friend died, thirsted, himself died, and these actions proved he was human. Human *and* divine, despite the fact that they were opposites. Actions proved it and thinking in terms of verbs made it possible to proclaim it.

Another example. What is man, good or evil, helpless or free? Greek philosophers have debated this issue, and chosen one side or the other. Thinking logically or consistently, they have maintained one point of view or the other but never both. From Plato of earliest times right on into the 20th century we find a stream of Greek-type thinkers saying that man is good, noble, free, and self-determining. Plato believed that, so did the philosophers of the French Enlightenment, so does Benjamin Spock. And so does modern day Communism as a philosophy. All of those interpretations of life begin on the assumption that man is good, noble, a free and exalted creature who will do what is right.

On the other hand, another stream of Greek-type philosophers argues in the other direction, insisting that man is not good but evil, not free but determined and helpless. Schopenhauer argued that man was evil. Spinoza argued that man was helpless and his life spelled out by arbitrary fate. Alongside Diderot and Voltaire and Rousseau of the French Enlightenment, all of them arguing that man was good, there was another Frenchman, de Sade by name, from whose name comes "sadism." De Sade argued that man was evil to the core, his basic instincts were to rape and to murder.

Greek thought always picks one side or the other, and therefore Greek logical consistent thought never has been able to fully understand both the mystery and grandeur of man. Only the Bible, thinking in Hebrew paradoxical thought, holding opposites together in tension, has the courage, audacity, and insight to affirm that both are true. Man is good, noble, an exalted and free creature. Man is evil, debased an enslaved creature. Both are true! Made in the image of God, sold into the bondage of the devil! Contradictory, but correct! One never will understand the fullness of the human personality until one holds these opposites together.

Jesus speaks of man's freedom, of man's ability to make decisions, by saying, "Take up your cross and follow me!" The very demand assumes ability to fulfill it. And yet, side by side with that affirmation of freedom, the Apostle Paul under the Spirit can write, "I can will what is right, but I cannot do it." Man is in bondage, a beast of burden made to be ridden and often unable to choose his own rider. The truth of man is not to be found in choosing one side or the other, but in maintaining both. I am a good man, aspiring to the stars, hungering for beauty and perfection, seeking the higher way. I am an evil man, debasing myself and harming those about me. I am free! I do make decisions, responsibly decide what I should do. I am helpless! I wake up to my actions with the sickening realization that I have done that which I did not want, and it is no longer I that do it.

The truth of man is not found in logical consistent Greek thought, which says with Plato or Communism that man is good. That is only half the truth, and hence half a lie. Nor is the truth of man to be found in the pessimism of Schopenhauer or the despair of de Sade which says I am evil and unredeemable. That is only half a truth, hence half a lie as well. The truth is found in Hebrew dialectical or paradoxical thought, able to balance opposite views together in delicate tension and affirm two contrary things simultaneously. I am good, of God; I am evil, of the devil.

When once one learns to think in these paradoxical terms, the problem we posed for ourselves at the outset of the chapter—how is it that Revelation can seem to contradict the apocalyptic views of suffering which are also seen in the Synoptic Gospels and in Paul—answers itself.

The writings of John reflect a different evaluation of life and emphasis on the work of Jesus from that found in the synoptics and Paul. The synoptic Gospels and Paul stress the apocalyptic views of demonology and eschatology. By that we mean that Paul and the synoptics stand in the apocalyptic stream of thought, stressing the revolt of Satan and his seizure of power in the immediate scene.

For example, Paul in his writings, refers to the devil, to the demonic principalities and powers, as the "world rulers of this present darkness" (Eph. 6:11-12). Because this world is dominated by Satan, Paul can call it the "present evil age" (Gal. 1:4). This is demonology, the basic belief that this world to some undefined degree is exposed to the malignant activity of God's enemy, the devil. Because Paul and the synoptics believe that, they can see the hand of the devil in all things causing pain and suffering. The tragedies and frustrations of this world are not the work of the Father in heaven, but the devil on earth. If Paul is unable to visit his congregation, he insists that it is Satan who is hindering him (1 Thess. 2:18). If he is ill he traces his affliction back not to God but to the devil (2 Cor. 12:7). Famine, hunger, persecution, all the tragedies of life seeking to separate us from God and shatter our hope, are tracked back to the powers and principalities, the demonic foes (Rom. 8:35, 38).

The synoptic Gospels have exactly the same stance. Suffering does not originate in God. It is opposed by God! Jesus, confronted by a crippled woman bent over near double with curvature of the spine, does not trace her illness back to some judgment of God. He flatly insists, on the contrary, that it was Satan who bound this woman in pain (Luke 13:16). All the miracles of Jesus show Jesus in opposition to the works of the devil. The people of that time believed that Satan caused hunger, and Jesus feeds the multitudes. The devil caused sickness, and Jesus heals the sick. This is the apocalyptic view that Satan is active, the "world ruler" of this present darkness, causing pain. This is demonology. And the synoptics especially are dominated by demonology. That is why the number one miracle, statistically, performed by Jesus is exorcism, the casting out of demons.

This belief, that Satan is active on the present scene, creates the apocalyptic hope for a future cleansed world. Demonology produces eschatology, the hope of the new future beginning. The devil is active in the present, but God will defeat him and restore his rule over all things. Thus we see all through Paul the forward look, the attitude of expectation, the yearning for that future intervention of God when he will come and destroy the devil and all his works and all his ways. That is seen in almost every letter of Paul. It is seen in 2 Thess. chapter 2. It is the subject of 1 Thess. chapter 4. It is stressed in Romans 8, 1 Cor. chapter 7. Indeed, in almost every letter of Paul we see that forward look, that eschatological look, where his eye is fastened on the horizon, awaiting that intervention of God in the future which will destroy the devil. God's hand is not in the present, but will be felt in the future. The synoptic Gospels have that same stance. In each of the synoptic Gospels we find extended discussion of the coming end of the world, the destruction of Satan's empire, and the creation of the new heaven and the new earth. Mark chapter 13 is one such chapter, Matthew 24 is another, Luke 12 and 21 yet others.

By way of summary, the primary thrust of apocalyptic thought, carried on into Paul and the synoptics, is the conviction that Satan has revolted and is active in the world. Suffering and pain and tragedy are traced back to him. The trials of this world are not the will of God but the work of God's enemies. God will act in the future and make all things right. This is why a chapter such as Romans 8 can be written. On the one hand, it is a catalog of agonies, a listing of the tribulations through which the church must pass . . . but there is no pessimism in it. Instead, there is the robust conviction that God will bring forth the victory and liberate the elect, that there is "nothing in all of creation" which can separate us from the love of God. God's way will win. The devil may rage, but God shall rule. Demonology is offset and overruled by eschatology. The present age may be evil, but a great day is coming. That is the hope, the promise, of apocalyptic and of the synoptics. God is stronger than any foe we face. The foes are real, the terrors great, but God is greater and thus there is rejoicing.

But John represents a different point of view. For John suffering is not traced back to the enemy of God, Satan, but to God himself. For John, both in the Gospel of that name and in the book of Revelation, there is no such thing as true demonology. John does not regard Satan as an independent enemy exerting his own malignant will. Satan is but a servant. God is the source of all things, including suffering. Suffering is not a work of the devil, but a judgment of God. This we have seen to be true all through the book of Revelation, and it can easily be seen in the Gospel of John as well.

Read, for example, John 5:14, and compare and contrast it to Luke 13:16. In Luke 13:16, as we have seen, Jesus sees suffering as caused by the devil, and liberates the woman from her illness. But in John 5:14 suffering is seen as coming from God, and the healed man is solemnly warned to sin no more lest something worse befall him.

In the Gospel of John, there is no demonology, no affirmation of Satan as existing as an independent foe. Instead, in the two places in the Gospel where Satan is specifically mentioned (John 12:31, 16:11), he is described as already defeated, now cast down, judged, and controlled even then. And that is why there is no case of exorcism, of casting out demons, in the Fourth Gospel! There is no demonology, no affirmation of the independent existence of Satan operative as an enemy of God, neither in the Gospel nor in Revelation.

And just as demonology is omitted, so also eschatology has faded. John does not look for the hand of God in the future. He sees it in the present. We have seen that fact again and again as we pored over Revelation. And the same fact can be seen in the Gospel of John as well. Whereas the synoptic Gospels think eschatologically and expect the final intervention of God, his ultimate judgment, to come at the end of time, the Gospel of John instead insists that it is going on right now, in the present. John 3:18 insists, "He who believes in him is not condemned; he who does not believe is condemned *already*. . . . "

This is, of course, over-simplification to a certain extent, and an entire book would have to be written to clarify all the details and fine points. Nonetheless it can clearly be maintained that there is a fundamental and far-reaching difference in attitude and interpretation between John on the one hand, and the synoptics and Paul on the other. The one side is apocalyptic, stressing demonology and eschatology, whereas the other is not. Suffering for one side is demonic, for the other side it originates in God. God's power for one side is future, to be seen at the end of time. For the other, God is active and present even now.

There is a difference of emphasis here, and thus we are forced to ask, "Is Scripture in conflict with itself? Which point of view is correct? Is God active now, or only in the future? Is suffering good, beneficial, a just judgment of God, or is it diabolical, life-perverting, an affliction not of God but of Satan?"

The very fact that we ask the question at all reveals merely how enmeshed we are with Greek thought. The Bible is Hebrew. The Bible holds opposites together in tension. *Both* are true. God does act now—and in the future. Suffering can be good—or evil. Both aspects or ideas are true, and the synoptic Gospels stress one side, whereas John emphasizes the other.

Surely all of us can recognize that there are times when suffering is demonic, of the very essence of the devil himself. Surely there are times when each one of us have had the ripping red hands of arbitrary caprice shatter our hopes and destroy our dreams, when a senseless act of undeserved suffering sears our lives. A loved one, consecrated to God, killed in an automobile accident. A good man, living for Jesus, killed by lightning An innocent child who has done no wrong born with brain damage and doomed to be a human vegetable. Polio, cancer, earthquakes, floods. Is there a human who has not cried out in the agony of the psalmist, "How long, O Lord, how long?" Is there a human—I know not one—who has been exempted from the senseless frivolity of pain that shatters our goals and smashes our aspirations. How does one explain the butchery of Dachau, Bergen-Belsen, or Auschwitz? How does one deal with earthquakes and sickness, of tornadoes and typhoons, and square them with the conviction that God is both all-powerful and all-loving? There is no way! Those things are in direct opposition to the claim of the church that God is love. How love, if he maims unfairly and cripples at random? And causes gas furnaces to cremate an entire people? Most biblical authors rise up in wrathful rejection of a view that would trace these tragedies back to God, and insist that this is not the work or will of God but the work of God's enemy, Satan, and God shall destroy that foe.

But that does not exhaust the fact of suffering. The other side is also true. Who can deny that suffering can often be seen as the just result of an evil life? Who can deny that in many cases we have reaped what we have sown? If we are evil, since God is just, we bring judgment down on our heads. There are indeed times when tragedy and trial, though unwanted, must be acknowledged as fair, and aimed at a positive purpose. Each of us who have reared a child have often raised our hand in punishment. We afflict not to maim or cripple, but to control, curb, and create higher goals. We punish our child who runs into the crowded street at age three, but we punish him not to hurt him, but to protect him from harm, to make him shun the places where he can be destroyed. Suffering can have a positive purpose.

The Bible thinks dialectically, paradoxically, affirming opposite truths. Suffering can be evil, of the devil. Suffering can be good, of God. The synoptics and Paul and the apocalyptic period stress the one side. But John and the book of Revelation emphasize the other. The truth is to be found not in setting one side against the other as contradictory, but rather in holding them both together as complementary.

And this brings us to the second question we raised at the outset of this chapter. How can we see the emphasis of Revelation—God punishing his people—as consistent with our idea of God as love, compassionate, and concerned?

The question can only be asked by those who have misunderstood what love is, and have dissolved religion into a caricature. For many, love has been diluted into indulgence. It is assumed that since God loves us, he will spare us all trial. It is assumed that religion means freedom from all pain, a celestial aspirin tablet prescribed by the Great Physician exempting us from all suffering. That is simply not true. Life begins in pain, as any mother can tell us, and life matures in suffering. Suffering can be positive, can produce growth and character. Jesus was love, but he was also strong and sharp and stern and bracing, a bare-knuckled and bronzed warrior who knew how to be firm and when to discipline and when to upbraid and scold.

Because God is love, it does not follow that religion means freedom from all trial. The line found early in Revelation, "Those whom I love, I reprove and chasten" (Rev. 3:19), is not only a key to the entire book of Revelation. It is also a depiction of an entire attitude toward life and toward suffering. Whereas the synoptics and Paul can stress, under the Spirit, that suffering is often inexplicable and diabolical, John, under the Spirit, reminds us of the contrary but complementary truth—that sometimes in sufferings laid on us by God we find the very love of God most actively revealed.

We began this book by insisting that the writing of

Revelation can best be understood by comparing it with the prophet Daniel. The style of writing of the one helps explain the other. And that is true. But only to an extent. John's Revelation copies the style and form of Daniel. Just as Daniel was written in disguised and cryptic language to get past the censors and extend a message of comfort to a persecuted people, so also Revelation is written in disguised and symbolic language to pass the censors and extend a message of comfort to a persecuted people.

But there the similarity ends. Daniel was apocalyptic, insisting that the suffering of the people was the work of God-opposing forces, and God would rescue in the future. That was his message of hope. But Revelation, while it takes up the form of apocalyptic, abandons the content of Daniel. For Revelation, the suffering of the people was the will of God active in the present. How does *that* offer any comfort or hope?

The answer is found by recognizing that while John's Revelation might borrow its style or form from Daniel, it borrows its content or message of hope from two other prophets—Jeremiah and Ezekiel

Jeremiah is given a message of woe, of judgment. He is told to denounce the people and preach over their heads the message of impending judgment. A judgment which will come not from Satan, but from God himself. He will level their homes, incinerate their vineyards, drive them into exile. Jeremiah is aghast. He cries out, No! He will not do it! He will be still, speak no more! He wishes that his head were waters, his eyes a fountain of tears, that he might weep for the slain of his people. He finds God harsh, and resolves to keep silence. But he cannot be still. God forces him to speak.

And finally, in desperation, he complains directly to God, insisting that this is not fair. He challenges God. And the answer he gets ovehwhelms him, staggers him.

Instead of compassion and understanding from God, he is shouted down, told to shut up! To cease his whining and continue his message of woe. Things will get worse before they get better. "If you have raced with men on foot, and they have wearied you, how will you compete with horses? And if in a safe land you fall down, how will you do in the jungle of the Jordan?" (Jer. 12:5). Jeremiah, if you cannot even run with the footmen, how do you expect to keep up with the horses? If you cannot even stand in the puddles of your own despair, what will you do when the rivers of judgment are flowing in full torrent? Jeremiah, you have seen nothing yet. Go back to your message of woe! No God of indulgent permissiveness here. No aspirin tablet religion washing away our struggles. A harsh and stern picture of an avenging God who is determined to bring judgment, suffering on his people!

But finally, it soaks into Jeremiah's head, if *he* is capable of loving this wayward people, how much more God! If he can weep over their impending tragedy, how much more the God who created them. Astoundingly, as he is ordered to turn to his message of woe, he comes to see the purpose of that woe. God is chastising in order to heal, hurting to make whole. Out of the anguish comes purification. Jeremiah comes to see the flames of fury as an evidence of God's love, burning away impurity. Thus the climax of his book comes not in his depiction of woe, but in his affirmation of the positive purpose of that woe—that out of suffering will come renewal. Out of the exile, the battering of Babylon, will come a cleansed people consecrated unto God. The magnificent lines of Jeremiah are not the ones which concentrate on the calamities but on the renewal. "Behold I will gather them from all the countries to which I drove them in my anger and my wrath and in great indignation; I will bring them back to this place, and I will dwell with them in safety. And they shall be my people, and I will be their God. I will give them one heart and one way, that they may fear me for ever, for their own good, and the good of their children after them. I will make with them an everlasting covenant, that I will not turn away from doing good to them; and I will put the fear of me in their hearts, that they may not turn from me. I will rejoice in doing them good, and I will plant them in this land in faithfulness, with all my heart and all my soul" (Jer. 32:37-41).

The same message bubbles out of Ezekiel. Ezekiel was a cold man, harsh, rejoicing at the outset in his message of woe and impending suffering. He spoke to the same people, about the same time as Jeremiah, with the same message of impending suffering. The only difference was that Ezekiel at first appeared to enjoy the message of doom, whereas Jeremiah smarted under it. But at the moment that Ezekiel's message of doom is verified, vindicated in history, at the very moment that Jerusalem is falling, at precisely that same time, his wife dies.

And suddenly Ezekiel sees the deeper truth. If he can lose a wife and suffer pain, how much more will God himself grieve in losing an entire people! Even as the black smoke billows over Jerusalem, he buries his wife. His tongue cleaves to his mouth. He cannot speak, so great is his grief. But if he can yearn for the restoration of one woman, how much more the desire of God to restore an entire people. And suddenly Ezekiel's whole message alters. Now he sees the purpose of the pain. Now he sees the reason for the woes. God is not crushing to cripple. There is no joy in the heart of God in the sending of suffering, and thus there ought be no joy in the heart of the prophet raised up to announce suffering. And Ezekiel alters his attitude. In the second half of the book, his harshness is gone, and the compassionate concern of God is clearly proclaimed. There was a reason for the woe, and that reason was cleansing.

The powerful ability of Ezekiel to create compelling images, used so graphically in the first part of his book to evoke terror and despair of judgment, is now used to evoke images of hope and comfort. There appear the promises of the dry bones which will rise again. There appear the promises of a coming shepherd who will restore the flocks of God. Out of agony there comes cleansing. The Lord chastens those whom he loves. Out of persecution there comes perfection: "For thus says the Lord God: Behold I, I myself will search for my sheep, and will seek them out. . . . I will feed them with green pasture. . . . I myself will be the shepherd of my sheep, and I will make them lie down, says the Lord God. I will seek the lost, and I will bring back the strayed, and I will bind up the crippled, and I will strengthen the weak, and the fat and the strong I will watch over, I will feed them in justice" (Ezek. 34:11-16).

That is the thought of Revelation. That is John's message of hope and comfort. God's children are suffering not because God has abandoned them, but because he loves them. Out of their anguish will come their renewal